First World War
and Army of Occupation
War Diary
France, Belgium and Germany

23 DIVISION
69 Infantry Brigade
Alexandra, Princess of Wales's Own (Yorkshire Regiment)
8th Battalion
26 August 1915 - 31 December 1917

WO95/2184/2

The Naval & Military Press Ltd
www.nmarchive.com
Published in association with The National Archives

Published by

The Naval & Military Press Ltd

Unit 10 Ridgewood Industrial Park,

Uckfield, East Sussex,

TN22 5QE England

Tel: +44 (0) 1825 749494

www.naval-military-press.com

www.nmarchive.com

This diary has been reprinted in facsimile from the original. Any imperfections are inevitably reproduced and the quality may fall short of modern type and cartographic standards.

© Crown Copyright
Images reproduced by permission of The National Archives, London, England, 2015.

Contents

Document type	Place/Title	Date From	Date To
Heading	WO95/2184/2 8th Btn Yorkshire Reg 1915 Aug 1917 Oct		
Heading	23rd Division 69th Infy Bde 8th Bn Yorkshire Regt Aug 1915-1917 Oct to Italy.		
Heading	69/23rd Division 8th Yorkshires Vol I Aug To Oct 15 Feb 19		
Miscellaneous	Confidential War Diary Of 8th (Service) Battn Yorkshire Regiment From 26.8.15 To 31.10.15 (Volume)		
War Diary	Bramshott.	26/08/1915	26/08/1915
War Diary	Boulogne.	27/08/1915	27/08/1915
War Diary	Monnecove.	27/08/1915	05/09/1915
War Diary	Wallon-Cappel.	06/09/1915	06/09/1915
War Diary	Oultersteen	07/09/1915	12/09/1915
War Diary	Rue Del Pierre	13/09/1915	13/09/1915
War Diary	Billets. Rue Delpierre.	14/09/1915	14/09/1915
War Diary	Trenches (55-58).	15/09/1915	15/09/1915
War Diary	Rue Del Pierre	16/09/1915	16/09/1915
War Diary	Trenches. (55-58)	17/09/1915	26/09/1915
War Diary	S. Trenches.	26/09/1915	26/09/1915
War Diary	Rolanderie District.	26/09/1915	26/09/1915
War Diary	Fort Rompu.	26/09/1915	26/09/1915
War Diary	Rue Marle.	10/10/1915	10/10/1915
War Diary	Trenches. I.20.2. To I.21.3	11/10/1915	11/10/1915
War Diary	Rue Marle	15/10/1915	16/10/1915
War Diary	Trenches. 21.6 I 16	19/10/1915	19/10/1915
War Diary	Bois Grenier Lines.	23/10/1915	23/10/1915
War Diary	Trenches. 121.4-I 16	27/10/1915	27/10/1915
Heading	23rd Division 8th Yorkshires Vol: 4 Nov 15 121 7724		
War Diary	Fort Rompu.	02/11/1915	02/11/1915
War Diary	Trenches.	07/11/1915	07/11/1915
War Diary	Bois Grenier.	11/11/1915	11/11/1915
War Diary	Rue Marle.	12/11/1915	12/11/1915
War Diary	Trenches.	14/11/1915	14/11/1915
War Diary	Bois Grenier. Lines.	18/11/1915	18/11/1915
War Diary	Trenches.	22/11/1915	22/11/1915
War Diary	Rue Dormoire.	24/11/1915	24/11/1915
Heading	23rd Division 8th Yorkshires Vol 5 121/7911		
Heading	War Diary Of 8th. Yorkshire Regiment. From 6.12.15. to 29.12.15 (Volume.)		
War Diary	Rue Dormoire.	06/12/1915	06/12/1915
War Diary	La Rolanderie.	11/12/1915	11/12/1915
War Diary	I.32. to I.26.4	12/12/1915	12/12/1915
War Diary	La Rolanderie.	15/12/1915	18/12/1915
War Diary	T.I.32 to I.26.4	21/12/1915	22/12/1915
War Diary	Jesus Farm	22/12/1915	29/12/1915
War Diary	Rue Marle.	29/12/1915	02/01/1916
Heading	8th Yorkshires Vol: 6		
Heading	War Diary of 8th. Yorkshire Regiment. from 2nd. January 1916. to 31st. January 1916. (Volume .)		

Type	Location	From	To
War Diary	Rue Marle.	02/01/1916	02/01/1916
War Diary	Trenches.	06/01/1916	06/01/1916
War Diary	Rue Marle.	08/01/1916	10/01/1916
War Diary	Trenches.	11/01/1916	15/01/1916
War Diary	Fort Rompu.	17/01/1916	21/01/1916
War Diary	Trenches.I.32.I. To I.26.4	23/01/1916	27/01/1916
War Diary	Rolanderie.	27/01/1916	31/01/1916
War Diary	Trenches. I.32.I. to I.26.4	31/01/1916	31/01/1916
Heading	War Diary of 8th. Battalion Yorkshire Regiment. From. 1st. February 1916. to 28th. February 1916. (Volume.). & March 1-31		
War Diary	Trenches. I.32 to I.26.4	01/02/1916	01/02/1916
War Diary	La Rolanderie	02/02/1916	04/02/1916
War Diary	Hallobeau.	08/02/1916	14/02/1916
War Diary	Vieux Berquin.	14/02/1916	14/02/1916
War Diary	Steenbecque	15/02/1916	25/02/1916
War Diary	Neuf Berquin.	25/02/1916	27/02/1916
War Diary	Steenbecque	28/02/1916	29/02/1916
War Diary	Ruitz.	01/03/1916	05/03/1916
War Diary	Servins.	06/03/1916	06/03/1916
War Diary	Souchez Sector.	07/03/1916	10/03/1916
War Diary	Gouay Servins.	11/03/1916	13/03/1916
War Diary	Bruay.	14/03/1916	18/03/1916
War Diary	Angres Sector.	19/03/1916	19/03/1916
War Diary	Trenches	20/03/1916	31/03/1916
Heading	War Diary of 8th (Service) Battalion (A.P.W.O.) Yorkshire Regiment. From-1st. April 1916. to 30th. April 1916 (Volume). Vol. 9		
War Diary	Angres III Sector	01/04/1916	30/04/1916
Heading	War Diary of 8th (Service) Battalion Yorkshire Regiment. From 1st May 1916 To 31st May 1916. Vol 8		
War Diary	Fosse 10	01/05/1916	18/05/1916
War Diary	Trenches	19/05/1916	20/05/1916
War Diary	Fosse 10	21/05/1916	26/05/1916
War Diary	Trenches	27/05/1916	31/05/1916
Heading	War Diary of the 8th (Service) Battalion, (A.P.W.O.) Yorkshire Regiment. From-1st June 1916-to-30th. June 1916. Vol. 9		
War Diary	Coupigny	01/06/1916	17/06/1916
War Diary	Estree Blanche	18/06/1916	30/06/1916
Heading	69th Inf. Bde. 23rd Div. 8th Battn. The Yorkshire Regiment. July 1916		
Heading	War Diary of 8th (Service) Battn Yorkshire Regiment from 1st July to 31st July 1916. Vol 10		
War Diary		01/07/1916	31/07/1916
Heading	23rd Division 69th Brigade. 1/8th Battalion Yorkshire Regiment August 1916		
War Diary	Albert	01/08/1916	31/10/1916
War Diary	Ypres	01/11/1916	04/11/1916
War Diary	Toronto Camp	05/11/1916	11/11/1916
War Diary	Trenches	12/11/1916	16/11/1916
War Diary	Ypres	17/11/1916	22/11/1916
War Diary	Toronto Camp	22/11/1916	30/11/1916

Heading	War Diary of 8th (Service) Battalion A.P.W.O. Yorkshire Regiment 1st December 1916 to 31st December 1916. Vol 15		
War Diary	Trenches	01/12/1916	03/12/1916
War Diary	Ypres	04/12/1916	07/12/1916
War Diary	Trenches	08/12/1916	11/12/1916
War Diary	Ypres	12/12/1916	15/12/1916
War Diary	Toronto Camp	16/12/1916	23/12/1916
War Diary	Trenches	24/12/1916	27/12/1916
War Diary	Bund	28/12/1916	31/12/1916
War Diary	Trenches	01/01/1917	04/01/1917
War Diary	Bund	05/01/1917	09/01/1917
War Diary	Toronto Camp	10/01/1917	16/01/1917
War Diary	Infantry Barracks	17/01/1917	20/01/1917
War Diary	Trenches	21/01/1917	24/01/1917
War Diary	Infantry Barracks	25/01/1917	28/01/1917
War Diary	Trenches	29/01/1917	31/01/1917
War Diary	In The Field	01/02/1917	28/02/1917
Heading	War Diary of 8th (Service) Battalion A.P.W.O. Yorkshire Regiment 1st March 1917 to 31st March 1917 Vol 18		
War Diary	Field	01/03/1917	31/07/1917
Heading	War Diary of 8th (Service) Battalion. A.P.W.O. Yorkshire Regiment. 1st August 1917 to 31st August 1917. Vol 73		
War Diary	In The Field	01/08/1917	31/08/1917
Heading	8th Yorkshire Regiment. War Diary for September 1917. Vol 24		
War Diary	Field	01/09/1917	30/09/1917
Heading	8th. Service Battalion A.P.W.O. Yorkshire Regiment. War Diary October 1917. Vol 25		
War Diary	In The Field.	01/10/1917	31/10/1917
Miscellaneous	Cittadini	28/11/1917	28/11/1917
Miscellaneous	Felow-Citizens	28/11/1917	28/11/1917
Miscellaneous	To My British And French Comrades		
Miscellaneous			
War Diary	Edifizio	01/12/1917	01/12/1917
War Diary	Montello Sector	02/12/1917	15/12/1917
War Diary	Montello Sector	03/12/1917	16/12/1917
War Diary	Venegazzu	17/12/1917	31/12/1917
Miscellaneous	69th Infantry Brigade. Special Order Of The Day.	31/12/1917	31/12/1917
Miscellaneous	XIV Corps G61/12 23rd Division G24/8/4	27/12/1917	27/12/1917

WO 95 2184/2

8th Bn Yorkshire Reg

1915 Aug

1917 Oct

23RD DIVISION
69TH INFY BDE

8TH BN YORKSHIRE REGT
AUG 1915 - FEB 1916

1917 OCT

TO ITALY

1.2.
Cabinet

121/7595.

69/23 not known

8th Yorkshires
roe £2.3.4

Aug 10 Oct 15
Feb 19

CONFIDENTIAL.

War Diary
of.
(Service) 8th Yorkshire Regiment.

From 26.8.15. to 31.10.15.

(Volume   )

Army Form C. 2118.

WAR DIARY
or
INTELLIGENCE SUMMARY.
(Erase heading not required.)

Instructions regarding War Diaries and Intelligence Summaries are contained in F.S. Regs. Part II. and the Staff Manual respectively. Title pages will be prepared in manuscript.

Place	Date	Hour	Summary of Events and Information	Remarks and references to Appendices
BRAMSHOTT.	26.8.15. 24/8/15	4.15 pm.	The Battalion (less Transport and Machine Gun Section who had left at 1.15am. that morning) left BRAMSHOTT CAMP for entrainment to FOLKESTONE Harbour. The Battalion marched to LIPHOOK station in two parts (Q) Headquarters and C & D Coys. (2) A & B Coys. On arrival at FOLKESTONE HARBOUR at 9.45 pm. H.Q.s. and C & D Coys. embarked forthwith and arrived without incident at BOULOGNE HARBOUR at 11.20 pm.	
BOULOGNE.	27/8/15	12.30 am.	C and D Coys. arrived shortly after midnight and the entire Battalion marched out to the rest camp about 2½ miles distant, arriving at about 2.30 am.	
BOULOGNE.	27/8/15	3.15 pm.	The Battalion marched out from Camp at 3.15 and entrained for WATTEN : the transport and M.G. section was arrived on the train. WATTEN was reached at 9.45 pm. and after detrainment the Battalion marched to billets at MONNECOVE about 6 Kilometres distant.	
MONNECOVE.	27/8/15 to 5/9/15		The Battalion remained in billets at MONNECOVE during this period. Training consisted of Route marches, tactical exercises and general preparation for Trench Warfare. Details of Officers and O.R.s were sent to Machine Gun and Bombing Classes in the vicinity.	
MONNECOVE.	5/9/15	9.15 am.	The Battalion marched our from MONNECOVE and arrived at new billets at WALLON CAPPEL about 3 pm. Route via St.OMER and ARQUES. The march was 17 miles over very indifferent roads and the weather exceptionally hot, in consequence a large number of men fell out but all were reported present that night.	
WALLON-CAPPEL.	6/9/15		The Battalion left for fresh billets in the vicinity of VIEUX BERQUIN at 9.30 am. Route via HAZEBROUCK distance 14 miles. Conditions of march equally unfavourable. Billets near OULTERSTEEN were reached at 3.15 pm.	
OULTERSTEEN	7/9/15		Battalion was inspected at 5 pm. by Lieut.Gen.PULTENEY who complimented them on their appearance in the course of a short address.	
"	8/9/15		Battn. remained in billets at OULTERSTEEN.	
"	12/9/15		Battalion marched to new billets in RUE DELPIERRE a distance of about 4 Kilometres south of ERQUINGHEM. Route via STEENWERCK – CROIX du BAC – ERQUINGHEM.	
RUE DELPIERRE	13/9/15		Headquarters, Coy.Commanders etc. visited trenches of 2nd. CAMERON HIGHLANDERS. A general inspection of the trenches was made, the party returning to RUE DELPIERRE at 2 pm. The Camerons had been shelled heavily at 5 am.	

(2) Army Form C. 2118.

WAR DIARY
or
INTELLIGENCE SUMMARY.
(Erase heading not required.)

Instructions regarding War Diaries and Intelligence Summaries are contained in F.S. Regs., Part II. and the Staff Manual respectively. Title pages will be prepared in manuscript.

Place	Date	Hour	Summary of Events and Information	Remarks and references to Appendices
Billets. RUE DELPIERRE.	14-9-15	5 p.m.	Headquarters and A and B Coys. went into the trenches of the 2nd. CAMERONS for instructional purposes. Everything quiet.	
Trenches (55-58).	15-9-15	6 p.m.	A and B Coys. evacuated trenches and were relieved by C and D Coys. Headquarters and A and B Coy. returned to RUE DELPIERRE. Casualties 1 O.R. Wounded.	
RUE DELPIERRE.	16-9-15		Headquarters A and B Coys.relieved 2nd. Camerons in the trenches. Relief completed by 10 pm. Casualties 2/Lieut. W.V. FENTON seriously wounded. 1 O.R. Wounded.	
Trenches (55-58).	17-9-15		Nothing unusual occurred except intermittent shellings on each side. Casualties 2/Lieut.Fenton died of wounds. 1 O.R. Wounded 18th. 1 O.R.Killed and 1 wounded 19th.	
"	20-9-15 / 9-1-9-15		The day was marked by renewed activity all along the 4th line by our Artillery. The enemy did not reply to any extent. Casualties 1 O.R. Wounded.	
"	21-9-15		Between these two dates our Artillery constantly shelled the enemy's parapet and S.Trenches. Casualties B O.R.Wounded and 1. Killed 22nd. 3 O.R.Wounded and 2 Killed 24th. inst.	
"	24-9-15 & 25-9-15		Intermittent bombardment of enemy's trenches continued with rifle and machine gun fire. The enemy at once replied and shelled our trenches heavily for about 35 minutes doing very little damage. All repairs to parapet were completed in a few hours. During the day news of our general advance in the south was received and orders received to keep up intermittent outbursts of fire throughout the day. Casualties. 1 O.R.Killed and 1 wounded.	
"	26-9-15		The day was very quiet until about 5.30 pm. when enemy opened fire on trenches with heavy guns (probably 5.4. howitzers) firing about 20 rounds. No damage done. Casualties Nil. At 4.30 am. the enemy bombarded our trenches for about 25 minutes.	
Trenches (55 - 58).		7.30 p.m.	The Battalion was relieved in trenches by 9th.Yorkshire Regt.and proceeded ro reserve trenches in BOIS-GRENIER Lines. Casualties. 2/Lieut.C.J.W.Crichton wounded. O.R. 1 Killed 3 wounded. The Battalion carried out work in BOIS-GRENIER Lines constructing additional dugouts etc.	
S.Trenches. La ROLANDERIE DISTRICT.			The Battalion moved into billets in the LA ROLANDERIE District. Working parties furnished for the BOIS-GRENIER Lines. Casualties. 2 O.R. Wounded 3rd.	
FORT ROLPU			The Battalion moved into rest billets at FORT ROMPU and together with 10th.W.Riding Regt.found the 23rd.Div. Reserve. Training in Bomb throwing,trench warfare and bayonet fighting,continued with route marches, was carried out. Working parties were furnished. 2/Lieuts.LARNER, OAKLEY, and WATSON, reported for duty on Oct.7th. and 2/Lieut.Blunden reported 9th.Oct.1915.	

WAR DIARY
or
INTELLIGENCE SUMMARY.
(Erase heading not required.)

Army Form C. 2118.

(3)

Place	Date	Hour	Summary of Events and Information	Remarks and references to Appendices
RUE MARLE.	10/15/14	5.30 pm	The Battalion moved into billets at RUE MARLE relieving the 8th. Yorks.& Lancs.Regt.	
Trenches. I.20.2. to I.21.3.	9/10/15	10 pm	The Battalion relieved the 118th.Sherwood Foresters and remained there for four days. Nothing unusual occurred during the period. Casualties Officers Nil. O.R. 3 Wounded 2 O.R.Killed.	
RUE MARLE.	16/10/15	7 pm.	The Battalion was relieved by the 9th.Yorkshire Regt. and marched to billets at RUE MARLE where it remained for four days during which period training was carried out and working parties furnished.	
Trenches. I.21.4.-I.16	19/10/15	7.30 pm.	Occupied trenches relieving 10th. West Riding Regt. Remained four days. Enemy was very quiet throughout the period. Casualties Officers. Nil. O.R. 3 Wounded.	
BOIS GRENIER Lines.	23/10/15	7 pm.	On relief by 2nd.East Lancs.Regt. the Battalion proceeded to take over reserve trenches relieving 9th.Yorkshire Regt. and occupied them for four days during which nothing of importance occurred. Work was carried out on the trenches and R.E. working parties furnished. Casualties Officers Nil. O.R. Nil.	
Trenches. I.21.4.-I.16	27/10/15	6 pm.	Proceeded to take over trenches from 2nd.East Lancashire Regt. and occupied them for four days during which nothing of importance occurred. Work carried out by day and night on trenches. Casualties Officers Nil. O.R. Wounded 5.	

M. Stokes
Lieut.Colonel.
Commanding 8th.Yorkshire Regiment.

2.2.
3 sheets

8th Yorkshires
Vol: 14

121/7724

23rd Stratton

Nov. 15

Army Form C. 2118.

WAR DIARY
or
INTELLIGENCE SUMMARY.
(Erase heading not required.)

Place	Date	Hour	Summary of Events and Information	Remarks and references to Appendices
Fort Rompu.	2/11/15		The Battalion moved into rest billets at Fort Rompu. Training in Bomb throwing and trench warfare and bayonet fighting, continued with route marches was carried out working parties were furnished.	
Trenches.	7/11/15		Proceeded to take over trenches from 2nd. East Lancashire Regt. and occupied them for 4 days during which nothing of importance occurred. work carried out day and night Casualties Officers nil. O.R. 4 wounded.	
Bois Grenier. Rue Marle.	11/11/15 12/11/15		Battalion moved into Bois Grenier lines for one night. The Battalion moved into billets at Rue Marle. On the 13th inst. there was an accident at the Brigade Bomb School in which 4 men of this Battalion were injured.	
Trenches.	14-11-15		The Battalion proceeded to take over trenches from 2nd. East Lancs. Regt. and occupied them for 4 days. Nothing unusual occurred during that period Casualties Officers nil O.R. 3 wounded and 1 killed.	
Bois Grenier. Lines.	18-11-15		On being relieved the Battalion proceeded to take over the reserve trenches. during which period nothing unusual occurred. work was carried out on the trenches and R.E. working parties were furnished. Casualties Officers nil men nil.	
Trenches.	22-11-15		Proceeded to take over trenches from 10th. W. Riding Regt. and occupied them for 2 days Nothing of importance occurred during that period. Work was carried out on the trenches generally. Casualties Officers 1 wounded O.R. nil.	
Rue Dormoire.	24-11-15		The Battalion moved into rest billets at Rue Dormoire, and with the remainder of the 69th. Brigade found the 23rd Div, 1 Reserve. Battalion schools for bomb throwers and machine guns and in addition training in musketry building revetments wearing tube helmets etc. was carried out. daily route marches were also done working parties were found almost daily. 2/Lieut reported for duty on 25th. November.	

23ᵗᵉʳ Kurraun

Sh Yakshuri's
Vol #5

121/7911

K-c.

S. Z.
5 Khulo

S. Z.
5 Khulo

CONFIDENTIAL.

War Diary

of

8th. Yorkshire Regiment.

from 6.12.15. to 29.12.15.

(Volume .)

Army Form C. 2118.

WAR DIARY
or
INTELLIGENCE SUMMARY.

(Erase heading not required.)

Instructions regarding War Diaries and Intelligence Summaries are contained in F. S. Regs., Part II. and the Staff Manual respectively. Title pages will be prepared in manuscript.

Place	Date	Hour	Summary of Events and Information	Remarks and references to Appendices
RUB DORMOIRE.	6.12.15.	4pm.	The Battalion moved into billets in the ROLANDERIE district. The 69th.Brigade took over the right sector on this date. During the period at RUE DORMOIRE the training consisted of company drill, route marches, physical exercises, machine and bombing classes.	
LA ROLANDERIE.	11/12/15	4.15pm.	The Battalion relieved the 10th.W.Riding Regt. in the left subsection of the left sector. Training on the same lines as at RUE DORMOIRE was carried on at LA ROLANDERIE. Ontaking over, the trenches were in a very bad condition owing to the continuous rain and activity on the part of the enemy' artillery. The front parapet was down in several places and the communication and fire trenches full of water. The dispositions were two and a quarter companies in the firing line, remainder of the Battalion in the BOIS GRENIER Line.	
I.32. to I.26.4.	12/2/15		The parapet was repaired during the night of the 11th./12th. and parties were at work all day pumping out water. Casualties :- 1 killed, 1 wounded.	
LA ROLANDERIE.	15/12/15	6.0pm	The Battalion was relieved by the 10th.W.Riding Regt. and proceeded to billets in LA ROLANDERIE district. The period in the trenches was marked by general activity of the Artillery on both sides, no damage to an extent was done. The work carried out was confined to rebuilding the parapet and draining the trenches.	
LA ROLANDERIE. T.I.32 to I.26.4.	18/12/15	5.15pm	The Battalion relieved the 10.h.W.Riding Regt. in the left subsection.	
	21/12/15	6am	2/Lieut.B.G.Wellesley reported missing when out with a patrol opposite I.26.3. Casualties :- 3 wounded.	
ditto.	22/12/15	5.30pm	The Battalion was relieved by the Northumberland Fusiliers. During this period there was considerable activity on both sides. Our own artillery carrying out a fixed programme each day. All available working Parties were utilised for repairing the front line and communication trenches 2/Lieut. Wellesley was still missing when the Battalion left.	
JESUS FARM	22/12/15 to 26/12/15		The Battalion i.04 t5 BOIS & FARM between these two dates and carried out a daily programme of work.	

Army Form C. 2118.

WAR DIARY
or
INTELLIGENCE SUMMARY.
(Erase heading not required.)

Instructions regarding War Diaries and Intelligence Summaries are contained in F. S. Regs., Part II. and the Staff Manual respectively. Title pages will be prepared in manuscript.

Place	Date	Hour	Summary of Events and Information	Remarks and references to Appendices
JESUS FARM. (contd.)	22/12/15 to 30/12/15		consisting of route marches, musketry, machine gun classes etc., Working parties were furnished each day.	
RUE MARLE.	29/12/15	3.30 p	The Battalion took over billets from the 1st.Sherwoods.	
	2/1/16.			

R. F. Such
Major.
Commanding 8th.Yorkshire Regiment.

2353 Wt. W2344/1454 700,000 5/15 D. D. & L. A.D.S.S./Forms/C. 2118.

H. Z.
5 sheets

8th Yorkshire
Vol. 6

23d

CONFIDENTIAL.

War Diary

of

8th. Yorkshire Regiment.

From. 2nd. January 1916.   to 31st. January 1916.

(Volume .)

Army Form C. 2118.

WAR DIARY
or
INTELLIGENCE SUMMARY.
(Erase heading not required.)

Instructions regarding War Diaries and Intelligence Summaries are contained in F. S. Regs., Part II. and the Staff Manual respectively. Title pages will be prepared in manuscript.

Place	Date	Hour	Summary of Events and Information	Remarks and references to Appendices
RUE MARLE.	2/1/16.	5/-	The Battalion relieved the 11th.W.Yorkshire Regt.in the right section of the left sector. This period in the trenches was uneventful and quiet throughout. There were no casualties. The distribution of Companies was one company in BOIS GRENIER Line, two and three quarters coys. in front line and one platoon in support to the right company.	
Trenches.	6/1/16.	6.30/-	The Battalion was relieved by the 11th.W.Yorkshire Regiment and proceeded to billets in RUE MARLE. The usual programme of work was carried out and the various billets strengthened against shell fire.	
RUE MARLE.	8/1/16.	2.30/-	The G.O.C. 23rd.Division presented the ribbon of the D.C.M. to No.13873 Pte.CODLING for gallantry displayed when on patrol work on December 20th. and 21st.	
"	10/1/16.	11.30/-	The Battalion relieved the 11th.West Yorkshire Regiment in the right section. Casualties 1 wounded.	
Trenches.	11/1/16.		Col. Sir.W.BELLEW and Lieut.Col.FARRBL were attached to the Battalion for a three days tour of duty. Casualties 3 wounded.	
"	13/1/16.		Our artillery carried out a programme at 12 noon and 4.10 pm. About 100 H.E. were fired at various points in the enemy's parapet and support trenches at each of these times. The enemy retaliated and at 12.20 pm. shelled the Salient wounding eight men. Our front line and Battalion Headquarters were shelled at 4.15 pm. but there were no further casualties and very x little damage done.	
Trenches.	15/1/16.	5/-	The Battalion was relieved by the 11th.Northumberland Fusiliers and proceeded into Brigade Rest at FORT ROMPU.	
Fort Rompu.	19/1/16.		Lieut.Col.E.L.LOWDELL took over Command of the Battalion. Major R.LUSH rejoining the 11th.W. Yorkshire Regiment.	
" "	20/1/16.		Lieut.Col.E.L.LOWDELL proceeded to England on leave and Major LUSH took over command.	

Army Form C. 2118.

WAR DIARY
or
INTELLIGENCE SUMMARY.
(Erase heading not required.)

Instructions regarding War Diaries and Intelligence Summaries are contained in F. S. Regs., Part II. and the Staff Manual respectively. Title pages will be prepared in manuscript.

Place	Date	Hour	Summary of Events and Information	Remarks and references to Appendices
FORT ROMPU	2/1/16		Major VAUGHAN 1st.Worcester Regt. took over Command of the Battalion.	
			During the period in rest the usual programme of work was carried out, also special Bombing and Wire Cutting parties were trained with a view to a possible raid. There were no casualties at FORT ROMPU.	
Trenches. I.32.1. to I.26.4.	23/1/16 25/1. 27/1.	8/p.m. 8.30/a.m.	The Battalion relieved the 2nd.NORTHANTS Regt. in the trenches. The day was quiet throughout. Casualties two killed and two wounded. Artillery were active on both sides but our trenches were not damged in any way. No casualties. The Battalion was relieved by the 10th.W.Riding Regt. and moved to billets in the ROLANDERIE district.	
Rolanderie.	27/1. – 31/1.		Nothing of importance occurred during the period. On the night of the 30th. the Battalion was warned to be in readiness to move at any moment as the 10th.W.Riding Regt. were sending a raiding party of 50 men across to the German Lines. The enemy however, had strong patrols out and the raid was apportigly cancelled.	
Trenches. I.32.1. to I.26.4.	31/1/16	6.30/p.m	The Battalion relieved the 10th West Riding Regiment in the trenches	

P.S.Snishor Capt + Adjt
for Major.
Commanding 8th.Y'kshire Regiment.

CONFIDENTIAL.

War Diary

of

8th. Battalion Yorkshire Regiment.

From. 1st. February 1916. to 28th. February 1916.

(Volume .)

& March 1 - 31.

Army Form C. 2118

WAR DIARY
or
INTELLIGENCE SUMMARY
(Erase heading not required.)

Instructions regarding War Diaries and Intelligence Summaries are contained in F.S. Regs., Part II. and the Staff Manual respectively. Title Pages will be prepared in manuscript.

Place	Date	Hour	Summary of Events and Information	Remarks and references to Appendices
	February.1916.			
Trenches. I.32 to I.26.4.	1st.		The day was exceptionally quiet throughout except for aeroplane activity. Casualties-two wounded. The period in this sector was quiet and uneventful. The distribution of companies was 3 Companies in the front line and one in the BOIS GRENIER Line. Casualties 3 O.Rs wounded.	
	2nd.		Lieut.Colonel Lowdell took over command of the Battalion.	
LA ROLANDERIE. 4th.			The Battalion was relieved by the 10th.West Riding Regt., and moved to billets in the ROLANDERIE district. Casualties 3 O.Rs wounded, one being a self-inflicted wound.	
HALLOBEAU.	8th. to 14th.		The Battalion was relieved by the 10th.Northumberland Fusiliers and proceeded into Divisional Reserve at HALLOBEAU taking over billets from the 12th.Durham Light Infantry. During this period the usual programme of work was carried out. In addition,both a Battalion Bomb and Machine Gun School were organised. On the 11th.February 1916 detailed orders were received for moving into Army Reserve at STEENBECQUE via VIEUX BERQUIN on the 14th.inst. A billeting party under Lieut.Pickering was told off to report to Staff Captain,102nd.Infantry Brigade at STEENBECQUE on 12th.inst in accordance with orders.	
VIEUX BERQUIN.	14th.		Battalion paraded at 8.45 a.m. and marched off at 9 a.m.They duly arrived at VIEUX BERQUIN and were all in billets by 3.45 p.m. There were no stragglers. Headquarters at Ferm B.17.d.8.5.	
STEENBECQUE.	15th.		The Battalion marched to STEENBECQUE arriving there at 12.30 p.m. Experienced some trouble in obtaining billets. Remainder of the day was spent in unloading kit and arranging billets. Casualties Nil.	
ditto.	16th.		Usual programme of work carried out. Bathing and Sanitary Conveniences were bad. Steps taken to remedy this. Casualties nil.	
ditto	17th.		Usual programme of work carried out. In addition running parade a.15 to 7.45 a.m. Lieut.M.G. Hume-Wright posted to Battalion with effect from yesterday. Casualties nil.	
ditto	18th.		Usual programme of work. Casualties nil.	
ditto	19th.		Battalion paraded for a route march via THIENNES - AIRE - BOESENGHEM. Casualties nil.	
ditto.	20th.		Church parades. Casualties nil.	
ditto.	21st.		Brigade bombing and Machine gun courses commenced. Miniature range allotted to Battalion each day for a week.	

Army Form C. 2118

WAR DIARY
or
INTELLIGENCE SUMMARY

(Erase heading not required.)

Instructions regarding War Diaries and Intelligence Summaries are contained in F. S. Regs., Part II. and the Staff Manual respectively. Title Pages will be prepared in manuscript.

Place	Date	Hour	Summary of Events and Information	Remarks and references to Appendices
STEENBECQUE	February 1916. 22nd.		Battalion with exception of "B" Company went on a route march. Received wire from Brigade to be ready to move to ESTAIRES tomorrow. Casualties nil.	
ditto.	23rd.		Battalion marched to NEUF BERQUIN in a snowstorm. Short rifles and long bayonets were issued to the Battalion before moving off. Casualties nil.	
NEUF BERQUIN	25th.		The Commanding Officer and Company Commanders visited the trenches in front of LAVENTIE occupied by the 2nd. Middlesex Regt. Casualties nil.	
ditto.	27th.		The 69th. Brigade returned to its former billets at STEENBECQUE arriving at 3.15 p.m. At 6.15 p.m. orders were received from Brigade that all Battalions were to hold themselves in readiness to move at short notice. Casualties. nil.	
STEENBECQUE	28th.		At 12 noon orders were received that the Brigade would move by train the following day 29th.inst.	

Lieut.Colonel,

Commanding 8th.Yorkshire Regiment.

Army Form C. 2118

8 York Regt

WAR DIARY
or
INTELLIGENCE SUMMARY
(Erase heading not required.)

Instructions regarding War Diaries and Intelligence Summaries are contained in F.S. Regs., Part II. and the Staff Manual respectively. Title Pages will be prepared in manuscript.

Place	Date	Hour	Summary of Events and Information	Remarks and references to Appendices
Steenbecque	29-2-'16	7.30am	Orders were received at 5.30 a.m. that the Brigade would move at 8 a.m. The Battalion entrained at Steenbecque Station at 8.30am. and detrained at CAMBLAIN CHATELAINE AT 10.10 am. The destination RUITZ was reached at 1 pm. distance about 6 miles. The 8th and 9th Yorks were billetted together taking over from the 1st K.R.R. The transport which came by road arrived at 6 p.m.	
RUITZ.	1-3-16		The day was spent in general cleaning up of equipment, and musketry.	
	2-3-16		The Battalion was inspected at 10.30 am. by the Corps Commander 4th Corps, Lieut-General Wilson.	
	3-3-16		The Battalion carried out the usual training viz:- Company and platoon drill, musketry etc.	
	4-3-16		Company Commanders visited the trenches in the SOUCHEZ Section which they were about to take over.	
	5-3-16			
SERVINS.	6-3-16	9.0m	The Battalion marched to billets in the SERVINS district. Headquarters and two companies were situated at GOUAY SERVINS, the remainder of the Battalion at PETIT SERVINS. Orders were received that night that the Battalion would take over the centre sector of the Brigade frontage the following day.	
SOUCHEZ Sector.	March 7th '16	4 pm	The Battalion on left GOUAY SERVINS in a snowstorm for the trenches. The French were relieved without casualities at 3 a.m.	
	8th		The enemy's artillery were very active during the morning. Aerial torpedoes were used against our front line.	
	9th		The day was quiet on the whole. Our front trenches were shelled at about 8.30 a.m. resulting in three casualities. Lieut-Col. T.S. Lambert took over command of the 69th Brigade.	
	10th		Intermittent shelling took place throughout the day. At 9 pm. the Battalion was relieved by the 2nd East Lancashire Regt., and proceeded to billets at GOUAY SERVINS.	
GOUAY SERVINS.	11th		These two days were spent in a general cleaning up of men and equipment.	
	12th		Orders were received on the 12th to march the following day to billets at BRUAY.	
	13th	12 noon	The Battalion marched to BRUAY arriving there at 5 p.m.	
BRUAY.	14th/15th		Company and platoon training was carried out and Baths allotted to the men.	
	16th		The G.O.C., Brigade inspected the Battalion, Transport lines and billets during the morning.	
	18th		The Battalion left BRUAY at 12 noon and marched to billets at HERSIN.	
ANGRES SECTOR.	19th	3.30 pm	The Battalion relieved the 24 Royal Fusiliers in the left subsection of ANGRES III Sector. The relief was carried in daylight without any casualities. The first company left HERSIN at 9.30 am.	

1875 Wt. W593/826 1,000,000 4/15 J.B.C. & A. A.D.S.S./Forms/C. 2118.

Army Form C. 2118

WAR DIARY
or
INTELLIGENCE SUMMARY

(Erase heading not required.)

Instructions regarding War Diaries and Intelligence Summaries are contained in F. S. Regs., Part II. and the Staff Manual respectively. Title Pages will be prepared in manuscript.

Place	Date	Hour	Summary of Events and Information	Remarks and references to Appendices
ANGRES SECTOR. Trenches	March. 19th	cont'd	The enemy were active during the afternoon especially with rifle grenades. Casualties three wounded	
"	20th		The enemy's artillery were very active throughout the day shelling our front line and support line morning and afternoon. At 3.5 p.m. we retaliated with Trench Mortars and artillery. As a result the enemy were quieter until about 7 p.m. They then opened a very heavy fire on the front line and Battalion Headquarters for half an hour, our artillery replied and by 7.45 p.m. all firing had ceased. Casualties five wounded.	
"	21st		The enemy were active with rifle grenades. Our Trench Mortars replied. Work on the trenches was hampered owing to difficulty in obtaining R.E. Material.	
"	23rd		Rain fell during the night, in consequence work was hindered, and men were employed in clearing the communication trenches. Casualties, one wounded.	
"	24th		The G.O.C., Division visited our lines. A heavy fall of snow during the night hindered work on the trenches. The two companies in the front line were relieved by the companies in local support and in reserve during the day. Casualties, two killed and three wounded. These men were hit by a rifle grenade at 5 p.m.	
"	25th	2 p.m.	The 68th Brigade carried out a demonstration with artillery, trench mortars and rifle grenades on our immediate left. The enemy did not retaliate on the lines. During the night there was a heavy fall of snow.	
"	26th		Intermittent shelling by the enemy throughout the day. We replied with rifle grenades. Casualties, nil.	
"	27th		During the morning our support company were heavily shelled. A machine gun was put out of action, the communication trenches damaged and two men were wounded.	
"	28th	3.20pm	A retaliation scheme was carried out with artillery, trench mortars, rifle grenades etc., on the enemy's front line.	
"	29th		The day was quiet throughout. Work was carried out on communication trenches, and support lines. Casualties nil. The G.O.C., Division visited the lines.	
"	30th		Companies in the front line were relieved. There was very little activity of any description on either side.	
"	31st	5:30am	The enemy's front line was fired on with Trench Mortars and rifle grenades. Very little retaliation resulted. Remainder of day was quiet. No Casualties.	

CONFIDENTIAL.

War Diary

of

8th (Service) Battalion (A. P. W. O.) Yorkshire Regiment.

From - 1st. April 1916. - - - - - - to - 30th. April 1916.

(Volume .)

Army Form C. 2118.

WAR DIARY
or
INTELLIGENCE SUMMARY.
(Erase heading not required.)

Instructions regarding War Diaries and Intelligence Summaries are contained in F. S. Regs. Part II. and the Staff Manual respectively. Title pages will be prepared in manuscript.

Place	Date	Hour	Summary of Events and Information	Remarks and references to Appendices
ANGRES Sector.	April 1916. 1st.		Night was generally quiet. At 9 pm. and 1 am. our artillery fired at points well behind of the enemy's lines. Intermittent shelling took place during the morning. The Battalion on our left is the 11th. Northumberland Fusiliers (68th. Brigade) on our right the 9th.Yorkshire Regt.	
	2nd.		Throughout the night transport could be heard in neighbourhood of ROLLENCOURT and LIEVIN. At 5.25 pm. a French aeroplane was brought down by German anti-aircraft guns about 600 yards in rear of Battalion Headquarters. Both occupants were killed and the machine wrecked.	
	3rd.		At 8 pm. there was intense artillery action in front of the SOUCHEZ sector. The Germans had shelled one of our Battalions during a relief and we retaliated with Howitzers for half an hour. Casualties 6 O.Rs. wounded.	
	4th. 5th. 6th.		The enemy shelled our lines with H.E. from 10.30 am to 11.45 am. Remainder of day was quiet. Nothing of importance occurred, the day being very quiet. Casualties Nil. Our artillery carried out a programme at 7.45 am. and 12.30 pm. There was practically no retalliation. Casualties NIL.	
	7th. 8th. 9th.		These days were quiet throughout, no casualties occurred.	
	10th.		The Brigade carried out a demonstration against the enemy's front and support lines. Our artillery opened fire at 1.30 pm. and fired salvos throughout the afternoon. At 4.29 pm. there was one minute of intense fire, the 68th.Bde. using smoke bombs. The operation ceased at 4.35pm. There was practically no retalliation. Casualties. 2 O.Rs. wounded.	
	11th. 12th. 13th. 14th.		Nothing of importance occurred. Casualties Nil. Everything quiet generally. On the latter day the enemy were active with Trench Mortars. Casualties O.Rs. 2 Killed and 1 wounded.	
	15th.		At 5.30 am. enemy shelled support line and Battn.Headquarters. No damage done. Casualties Nil.	
	16th.		At 2 pm. the Battalion was relieved by the 2nd.H.L.I. The enemy were active during the morning with rifle grenades. Billets at COUPIGNY were reached at 6 pm. Casualties O.Rs. 1 Killed and 4 wounded.	
	17th.		The Battalion left COUPIGNY at 12 noon and marched to billets at DIVION arriving there at 5 pm.	

Army Form C. 2118

WAR DIARY
or
INTELLIGENCE SUMMARY

(Erase heading not required.)

Instructions regarding War Diaries and Intelligence Summaries are contained in F.S. Regs., Part II. and the Staff Manual respectively. Title Pages will be prepared in manuscript.

Place	Date	Hour	Summary of Events and Information	Remarks and references to Appendices
	18th.		The day was devoted to bathing and general cleaning up of clothing and equipment.	
	19th.		The Battalion left DIVION at 8 am. and marched to billets at LAIRES a distance of about 20 kilometres for the manoeuvre period.	
	20th.		The Battalion marched to the manoeuvre area and the ground was reconnoitred in view of a Brigade Scheme to be carried out the following day.	
	21st.		The Battalion carried out an attack on the village of BOMY under the Brigade scheme.	
	22nd.		The day was devoted to internal economy and general cleaning up of equipment, clothing etc.	
	23rd.) 24th.) 25th.) 26th.)		These days were spent in Battalion training, Company and Platoon Drill etc. in the manoeuvre area.	
	27th.		The Battalion left the manoeuvre area, entrained at PERNES for BARLIN and from there marched to billets at FOSSE 10.	
	28th.) 29th.) 30th.)		The entire Battalion was employed on working parties on the MAESTRE Line and SOUCHEZ Sector. The Battalion was employed on working parties in the support line. Casualties Nil. Working parties were detailed each night. Musketry and Bayonet Fighting were carried out during the day. Casualties NIL.	

[signature]
Lieut. Colonel.

Commanding 8th (Service) Battalion Yorkshire Regiment.

8th York Reg
Vol 8

CONFIDENTIAL.

WAR DIARY

OF

8th (Service) Battalion Yorkshire Regiment.

From 1st May 1916.   To. 31st May 1916.

Army Form C. 2118

WAR DIARY
or
INTELLIGENCE SUMMARY
(Erase heading not required.)

Instructions regarding War Diaries and Intelligence Summaries are contained in F.S. Regs., Part II. and the Staff Manual respectively. Title Pages will be prepared in manuscript.

Place	Date	Hour	Summary of Events and Information	Remarks and references to Appendices
Fosse 10.	1st. 2nd. 3rd. 4th.		During the period the Battalion was billeted at FOSSE 10. Large working parties were furnished alternative days for work on the front and support lines. Musketry on a 30 yards range and the usual company training was carried out during the day.	
	5th.		The Battalion marched to billets at DIVION.	
	6th.		The Battalion was inspected at 9 a.m. by the G.O.C. 23rd.Division and afterwards attended a Gas Demonstration at HOUDAIN.	
	7th.		The Battalion carried out the usual programme of company and platoon work.	
	8th.		The G.O.C. 1st.Army attended Church Parade at 11 am.	
	9th. 10th.		These dates were devoted to training and working parties.	
	11th.		The Battalion left DIVION at 9 am. and marched to billets at COUPIGNY.	
	12th.		The Battalion left COUPIGNY at 9 am, and marched to BULLY GRENAY. A Coy. in billets at CORONS 11" AIX. B Coy. in Mechanics Trench. C Coy. and ½ D Coy. in Billets at BULLY Grenay and ½ D Coy. in trenches METRO CAP DE PONT. Casualties 1 O.R. wounded.	
	13th. to 17th.		Working parties were furnished daily to the Battalions in the front line. During this period all Companies with the exception of B Coy. bathed.	
	17th & 18th		The Battn. relieved the 9th.Yorks.Regt. in ANGRES 2 Sector. The enemy were fairly quiet except against M.20.1 when in the morning they were active with rifle grenades and trench mortars. Our T.M.Battery replied and silenced them. Casualties. 2 O.R.Killed and 1 O.R. wounded.	

Army Form C. 2118

WAR DIARY
or
INTELLIGENCE SUMMARY
(Erase heading not required.)

Instructions regarding War Diaries and Intelligence Summaries are contained in F.S. Regs. Part II. and the Staff Manual respectively. Title Pages will be prepared in manuscript.

Place	Date	Hour	Summary of Events and Information	Remarks and references to Appendices
Trenches.	19th.		At 5.58 am. we exploded a mine opposite M.20.1 and our artillery and trench mortars bombarded the enemy line. He retaliated with heavy trench mortars and 15 pounders on M.20.1. The other trenches were comparatively quiet. Casualties 7 O.R. wounded.	
"	20th.		The morning was on the whole quiet except as against M.20.1 when he was active with light and heavy trench mortars and rifle grenades. About 4.30 pm. a Trench Mortar duel was followed by a heavy enemy barrage of 15 pounders to 5.9" shells on our front and support lines. He did considerable damage to our front line and and support lines. During the night he was quiet. Casualties 1 O.R. wounded.	
Fosse 10.	21st.		About 10 am. the enemy continued his barrage of yesterday afternoon but did little damage. About 5 pm. we receive an alarm of gas and all the Battalion stood to for 2 hours. Gas was reported by the 68th.Brigade on our right. This proved to be false but the effect of tear shells was strongly felt. At about 8 pm. the alarm was repeated but was cancelled immediately. During the day the enemy consistently shelled the Battalion in our rear and Bully. The night was quiet casualties 7 O.R. wounded.	
"	22nd.		The Battalion was relieved by the 9th.Yorks.Regt. and proceeded to billets at Fosse 10. taking over from 10th.W.Riding Regt. Casualties 1 O.R. Killed.	
"			The enemy shelled Fosse 10 for 4 hours in the morning with 4.2", 5.9" and 8" shells. Casualties Nil. Working parties and usual cleaning up.	
"	24th.		Usual training carried on and working parties found for Town Major and front line. One man was hit on the Transport. Casualties 1 O.R.wounded. A.B and C Coys. bathed at Sains en Gohelle.	
"	25th.		Fosse 10 was quieter today Working parties were found as before. D Coy.bathed at BULLY GRENAY.	
"	26th.		The Battalion relieved the 9th.Yorks.Regt. in ANGRES 2 Sector. The day and night were quiet.	

1875 Wt. W593/826 1,000,000 4/15 J.B.C. & A. A.D.S.S./Forms/C. 2118.

Army Form C. 2118

WAR DIARY
or
INTELLIGENCE SUMMARY

(Erase heading not required.)

Instructions regarding War Diaries and Intelligence Summaries are contained in F.S. Regs., Part II. and the Staff Manual respectively. Title Pages will be prepared in manuscript.

Place	Date	Hour	Summary of Events and Information	Remarks and references to Appendices
Trenches.	27th.		The day was very quiet except for a little rifle grenade activity. The evening was quiet up to 10.30 pm. when an S.O.S message was received from the Brigade on our left. We stood to but everything was quiet on our front and subsequently the message "Cancel S.O.S" was received. Casualties Nil.	
	28th.		The day was fairly lively. There was a certain amount of activity on the part of the enemy with guns, trench mortars and rifle grenades. Our parapet was breached in several places. We retaliated with heavy trench mortars and rifle grenades. The night was quiet. Casualties 1 O.R. killed, 2 O.R. Wounded.	
	29th.		The day was quiet except for the usual exchange of T.M. and rifle grenades. The night was exceptionally quiet. Casualties Nil.	
	30th.		The Battalion was relieved by the 1st. Worcestershire Regt. and marched to billets at COUPIGNY. The men in huts and Officers in private billets. Casualties 2 O.R. wounded.	
	31st.		The usual training was carried out fresh clothing issued and the day was spent with inspections and cleaning up.	

JMMonk   Major.

Commanding 8th. Yorkshire Regiment.

8th York Reg
vol 9
June

WAR DIARY

of the

8th (Service) Battalion, (A.P.M.O.) Yorkshire Regiment.

From – 1st. June 1916. ———— To – 30th. June 1916.

Army Form C. 2118

WAR DIARY
or
INTELLIGENCE SUMMARY
(Erase heading not required.)

Instructions regarding War Diaries and Intelligence Summaries are contained in F. S. Regs., Part II. and the Staff Manual respectively. Title Pages will be prepared in manuscript.

Place	Date	Hour	Summary of Events and Information	Remarks and references to Appendices
Coppigny.	1st. June.		Bombing, Lewis Gun and Signalling Classes under the respective officers. The remainder of the Battalion paraded under Company arrangements. A working party of 1 N.C.O. and 20 men furnished to Town Major daily.	
	2nd.		The Battalion paraded for Church Service at the Y.M.C.A. Hut.	
	3rd.		Work carried on as on the 1st.with addition of daily practice in wiring.	
	4th. to 8th.		Battalion carried out the usual work programme with the addition of large working parties furnished nightly. During the period at COUPIGNY every effort was made to complete all kits & equipment and all men in the Battalion bathed.	
	8th.		The Battalion relieved the 13th.D.L.I. Regt. on LORETTE SPUR. Disposition of Companies as follows:- Left Company (B) (1) 3 Platoons at X.6.a.5.8. Centre Coy. (D) (1) 2 Platoons X5.d.7.2 (2) 1 Platoon at X.5.d.8.7. (2) 2 Platoons at X. Right Coy. (A) (1) 2 Platoons at X.11.d.9.9. Reserve Coy. at X.34.c.4½.5½. (2) 2 Platoons at X.5.d.4.5 Battn.Hd.Qr. at ABLAIN St.NAZAIRE.	
	9th.		The work on construction of deep dugouts was started and a party of 150 men was found nightly for the R.E. O.C. 128th.Field Coy.	
	10th.		Work continued.	
	11th.		Work continued. C and D Coys. of the 1st.Hanson Battn. R.N.D. and Hd.Qrs.relieved A and D Coys. and Hd.Qrs. of this Battn. and the command of Lorrette Spur was handed over to O.C.1st.Hanson Battn. A and D Coys. Lewis Guns remainded up. A and D Coys. and Hd.Qrs.moved to huts in BOUVIGNY Wood. Casualties 1 O.R. wounded.	
	12th.		The remaining 2 Companies on LORETTE SPUR viz - B and C Coys.and all Lewis Guns were relieved by the 8th.London Regt. and the whole Battalion moved back to Huts on the edge of BOUVIGNY WOOD.	
	13th.		The Battalion was relieved by the 23rd.Battn.London Regt.. They marched to billets at BRUAY. There were no stragglers.	
	14th.		The Battalion marched to billets as follows - Hd.Qrs. C and D Coys. at TANGRY. A and B Coys. at SAINS LES PERNES.	
	15th.		The day was spent in cleaning up and issuing clothing &c. to complete. Major P.K.Vaughan assumed command and Major J.M.Monk returned to his Regiment.	
	16th.		The Battalion marched to billets at ESTREE BLANCHE. There was one straggler. The Division become G.H.Q.Reserve from this date.	
	17th.		The Battalion carried out Company training &1. area.	

Army Form C. 2118

WAR DIARY
or
INTELLIGENCE SUMMARY
(Erase heading not required.)

Instructions regarding War Diaries and Intelligence Summaries are contained in F.S. Regs., Part II. and the Staff Manual respectively. Title Pages will be prepared in manuscript.

Place	Date	Hour	Summary of Events and Information	Remarks and references to Appendices
ESTREE BLANCHE.	18th.		Brigade Church parade and subsequently medals and decorations were presented by Major General J.M.Babington C.B., C.M.G. to No.12041 Pte.J.T.Wilkinson. "A" Coy. (Military Medal)	
	19th.		The Battalion took part in a Divisional Scheme of attack. Capt. B.C.M.WESTERN, 2nd. E.Lancs. Regt. arrived and took over the duties of 2nd.in Command.	
	20th.) 21st.) 22nd.) 23rd.)		The Battalion carried out Company training in the various sub-areas of the Special Manoeuvre Area.	
	24th.		The Battalion left ESTREE BLANCHE at 9 am. and marched to BERQUETTE where it entrained and 12.30 pm. for LONGEAU near AMIENS. On arrival at LONGEAU the Battalion marched to billets at BERTANGLES about 14 Kilometres distant, arriving there at midnight.	
	25th.) 26th.) 27th.)		These days were devoted to exterior economy and company training at BERTANGLES.	
	28th. 29th. 30th.		The Battalion went for a ten mile route march in Battle Order. The day was devoted to inspection of kits and interior economy.	

R Fyfe
Lieut.Colonel
Commanding 8th.Yorkshire Regiment.

69th Inf.Bde.
23rd Div.

8th BATTN. THE YORKSHIRE REGIMENT.

J U L Y

1 9 1 6

23/July

Vol 10.

War Diary of 8th (Service) Battn. Yorkshire Regiment.
From 1st July to 31st July, 1916.

Army Form C. 2118.

WAR DIARY
or
INTELLIGENCE SUMMARY.
(Erase heading not required.)

Instructions regarding War Diaries and Intelligence Summaries are contained in F. S. Regs., Part II. and the Staff Manual respectively. Title pages will be prepared in manuscript.

Place	Date	Hour	Summary of Events and Information	Remarks and references to Appendices
	July. 1st.		The Battalion moved to bivouacs in BAIZEUX WOOD arriving there at 12.20 p.m.	
	2nd.		The Battalion moved to bivouacs at ALBERT.	
	3rd.		The Battalion moved to bivouacs on TARA HILL.	
	4th.		The front line trenches opposite SAUSAGE REDOUBT were reconoitred and the same night "A", "B", & "C" Coys' dug a communication trench from the old British front line to SAUSAGE REDOUBT. "D" Coy were detatched for duty under O.C.9th.Yorkshire Regiment.	
	5th.		The 69th.Brigade attacked the German line ⊘ X21 a 49(incl.)X15 d.o.o X 21 b 38. X 22a 88 incl. The HORSESHOE line was to be captured, the line 79,85,74,& 33 was to be consolidated. The Battalion formed up(as part of the scheme) in front trenches of line SCOTS REDOUBT -27 and attacked front X d21 b 3.8.(excl.) to point X 21 b 74 (incl.). 4 M.G. were allotted to the Battn., and 2 Stokes Guns. Advance Bde.H.Q. was at SCOTS REDOUBT. The whole attack was quite successful.	

WAR DIARY
or
INTELLIGENCE SUMMARY.
(Erase heading not required.)

Army Form C. 2118.

Instructions regarding War Diaries and Intelligence Summaries are contained in F. S. Regs., Part II. and the Staff Manual respectively. Title pages will be prepared in manuscript.

Place	Date	Hour	Summary of Events and Information	Remarks and references to Appendices
	July. 6th.		The Battalion was relieved on this day by the D.L.I. 68th.Inf.Brigade and marched to Bivouacs at E 10 d.	
	7th.		The Battalion moved to bivouacs at Belle Vue Farm orchard to be in Divl. Reserve to the 24th. & 68th. Brigades.	
	8th.		The Battalion moved closer up to the trenches immediately in front of BECOURT WOOD. They were shelled fairly heavily that night. Casualties from and on the 5th. to this date were 3 Officers 'Wounded', 3 O.R. 'Killed', 1 O.R. 'Died of Wounds' 86 O.R's 'Wounded' and 1 O.R. 'Missing'.	
	9th.		This morning the Battalion was shelled severely, and Battalion H.Q. dugout was blown in. There were no casualties there. Later in the day the Battn. moved back to Belle Vue Farm to their former bivouacs.	
	10th.		The 69th.Inf.Brigade were ordered to attack and capture CONTALMAISON, with the 8th.Yorks.on the	

WAR DIARY

INTELLIGENCE SUMMARY.

(Erase heading not required.)

Army Form C. 2118.

Place	Date	Hour	Summary of Events and Information	Remarks and references to Appendices
			right, and the 9th.Yorks.on the left flank. The 11th.West Yorks.operating on the left of the 9th.Yorks., and protecting the flank. The Battalion advanced to the attack at 4-50 p.m.from the HORSESHOE TRENCH, and came under shrapnel fire from CONTALMAISON wood. As the Battalion further advanced and when within about 500 yds.from the village heavy machine gun and rifle fire was opened on them by the enemy from the front and left flank. On reaching TRENCH 22-41 the wire was found to be practically intact and provided a serious obstacle. After gaining this trench, where the men were still under heavy fire, the line advanced to the assault. A second obstacle in the shape of a hedge and wire netting held the line outside the village, and 50% of the casualties occurred between the trench and hedge. This obstacle was surmounted and the line advanced to the village firing at the enemy who were now retreating. At this point unexpected machine gun and rifle fire took the men in the rear and caused some casualties. Not more than 4 Officers and 15 150 men reached the village. 3 German officers and 160 men were captured exclusive of 100 wounded germans in dug-outs. 6 Machine Guns and thousands of rounds of ammunition were also taken. Immediate steps were taken to consolidate and a line was chosen that extended from the ⊠CHATEAU through the VIEUX MANOIR to point 84. It was not the best line for defense, but was selected in view of the small number of men available. By daylight the	

WAR DIARY
INTELLIGENCE SUMMARY.
(Erase heading not required.)

Army Form C. 2118.

Place	Date	Hour	Summary of Events and Information	Remarks and references to Appendices
			line was dug. At 7.30 p.m. a small party of Germans appeared at the CUTTING but were dispersed by machine gun (their own) fire. Our right was exposed and at 9 p.m. a party of about 40 Germans were seen to be lining the Hedge N. from Point 93. They opened fire and the position was critical. Major Western made a barricade across the road at 84, and was reinforced with more men from this and the 9th.Battn. The enemy were kept in check and finally dislodged by the further aid of a bombing party from the 9th. and A Lewis Gun fire from a house. At 11 p.m. the Battalion was reinforced by 2 Coys' of the 11th.West Yorks and the 10th.West Riding Battn. These got into touch with the unit on the right, and the position became satisfactory. The village was shelled all night, and during next day, but no counter attack was launched. Our patrols were out all night, and Boshe patrols in the CUTTING were fired on. 10th.Casualties:- Officers 5 Killed, 19 O.R's Killed, 6 Officers, 241 O.R's Wounded, 1 Officer and 67 O.R's Missing.	
	11th.		The Battalion was relieved that night, and marched to bivouacs at the same place in BELLE VUE FARM.	
	12th.		The Brigade moved to billets at FRANVILLERS for rest. The Battalion started at 11-15 a.m. No stragglers.	

Army Form C. 2118.

WAR DIARY
of
INTELLIGENCE SUMMARY.
(Erase heading not required.)

Instructions regarding War Diaries and Intelligence Summaries are contained in F. S. Regs., Part II. and the Staff Manual respectively. Title pages will be prepared in manuscript.

Place	Date	Hour	Summary of Events and Information	Remarks and references to Appendices
	13th.		The Brigade moved to billets at MOLLIENS AU BOIS arriving about 4-30 p.m. No stragglers.	
	14th.		The morning was spent in cleaning. In the afternoon the Battalion was inspected by the C.O. At 6 p.m. the Brigade paraded before the Divl. Commander who thanked them for their work on the 5th. and 10th. inst.	
	15th.		The Battalion paraded with the Brigade at the CHATEAU at MOLLIENS AU BOIS before the Corps Commander Lieut.General Sir W.P.Pulteney, when he thanked the Brigade for it's work.	
	16th.		The Battalion attended Church Parade at the CHATEAU at which the Divisional and Brigade Commanders were present.	
	17th.		The Battalion paraded under Company arrangements.	
	18th.		Early morning running parade, and subsequently under company arrangements. Draft of 7 men arrived.	

T2134. Wt. W708—776. 500000. 4/15. Sir J. C. & S.

Army Form C. 2118.

WAR DIARY
INTELLIGENCE SUMMARY
(Erase heading not required.)

9th/12 Yorkshire Regt. July 1916

951f

Place	Date	Hour	Summary of Events and Information	Remarks and references to Appendices
	19th.		Early morning parade running and physical drill under Company arrangements. At 9-45 a.m. The Battalion paraded and bathed at BERNCOURT. In the afternoon the men who had not bathed in the morning bathed. At 4-00 p.m. a lecture on Gas was given by Lieut. FARROW, 4th. Army Gas Expert.	
	20th.		Battalion went for route march. Afternoon, Interior Economy and Training of specialists. Draft of NM 32 men arrived.	
	21st. HQ		The Battalion moved to bivouacs at MILLENCOURT arriving about 2-30 p.m. Draft of 197 N.C.O's & men arrived about 7 p.m.	
	22nd.		Medical Inspection of drafts, and refitting them.	
	23rd.		Brigadier inspected the new draft a.m. Battalion paraded for Church Parade.	
	24th.		Battalion paraded under Company arrangements at 7-30 a.m. Physical Training etc. Battalion Sports in the afternoon.	

T2134. Wt. W708—776. 500000. 4/15. Sir J. C. & S.

Army Form C. 2118.

WAR DIARY
or
INTELLIGENCE SUMMARY.
(Erase heading not required.)

9524

Place	Date	Hour	Summary of Events and Information	Remarks and references to Appendices
	25th		Parades under Company arrangements. Div. Gas Expert inspected gas helmets in p.m.	
	26th		Battalion moved to billets in ALBERT, 10-30 a.m.	
	27th		The enemy shelled ALBERT intermittently during the day. Gas helmet parade, and several officers were sent to reconnoitre the position in the support lines. Casualties 2 O.R's 'Wounded'.	
	28th		The Battalion relieved the 10th.N.F. in trenches in and about PEAKE WOOD. Situation quiet. Working party of 400 men found to dig Yorkshire Trench. Casualty 1 O.R. 'Wounded'.	
	29th		Working party of 200 men to carry on with YORKSHIRE TRENCH. This night another large working party was found to dig trench in front of LANCS TRENCH. This was found to be impossible owing to attack by 10th. West Riding Regt., and enemy shelling consequent upon it. The enemy sent over a large number of gas shells the effects of which were felt strongly. 1 Officer slightly wounded at duty. 6 O.R's 'Wounded'.	

WAR DIARY
INTELLIGENCE SUMMARY.
(Erase heading not required.)

Army Form C. 2118.

Place	Date	Hour	Summary of Events and Information	Remarks and references to Appendices
	30th.		A party of 200 men from 68th.Brigade, and 150 from 9th.S.Staffords under Major Western and Capt. Player worked at the trench in front of LANGS TRENCH, and to the left of it. The enemy did not permit much work to be done. Casualties 3 O.R's 'Wounded', 1 O.R. Shell-shock.	
	31st.		A working party of 280 men dug 8th.Alley from CONTALMAISON VILLA to YORKSHIRE TRENCH, and worked on the latter trench. Casualties - Nil.	
	4.8.16			Bangham H.C.L. Cmdg. 8 Yorks.

9534
RB

23rd Division
69th Brigade.

1/8th BATTALION

YORKSHIRE REGIMENT

AUGUST 1 9 1 6

Army Form C. 2118.

10.2.
6 sheets

939 F SB

8 Yorks Regt

Vol II

WAR DIARY
or
INTELLIGENCE SUMMARY.
(Erase heading not required.)

Instructions regarding War Diaries and Intelligence Summaries are contained in F.S. Regs., Part II. and the Staff Manual respectively. Title pages will be prepared in manuscript.

1916

Place	Date	Hour	Summary of Events and Information	Remarks and references to Appendices
Albert	1st Aug		The Battalion relieved 10th W. Riding Regt. in Scott. Redoubt and under orders of 68th Inf. Brigade. Casualties 1 O.R. killed 5 Wounded Shell Shock.	
	2nd		The Battn. found working party of 100 men to proceed with Yorkshire Trench. Trench material carried.	
	3rd		The Battn. proceeded after being relieved by 10th W. Ridings to billets in Rue Reformer Albert.	
	4th		The men rested & bathed.	
	5th		The Battn. relieved the D. & I. 68th Brigade in the line in front of the Switch. So soon had we got in than the C.O. & Lieut. of Tilly were wounded & Major R.C.M. Winslow down a dugout. The enemy kept up a very heavy barrage all night & at 3.30 am & noon made two determined attacks on the Grenade Alley Post. These were both broken off by the occupants of the Post, who displayed great coolness.	
	6th		The Battn. received orders to attack & capture about 100 yards of Grenade Alley at 4.30pm, & to clear Torr Trench. The Leamis had been bombarding Tarr Trench & Grenade Alley up to the limit & the howitzers were bombarding the Switch Line for 2 hours on the morning & since 3pm in the afternoon. The scheme was for a Platoon to attack overland from O.G.2 a little to the right of Pt. 41 & simultaneously the Grenade Post occupants were to start bombing up Grenade Alley. At 4.30pm the attack was made & proved quite successful in first objective	

Army Form C. 2118.

WAR DIARY
or
INTELLIGENCE SUMMARY.
(Erase heading not required.)

Instructions regarding War Diaries and Intelligence Summaries are contained in F. S. Regs., Part II. and the Staff Manual respectively. Title pages will be prepared in manuscript.

Place	Date	Hour	Summary of Events and Information	Remarks and references to Appendices
	7th.		men was genuine than was acted for. A double flock was right will above the junction of Ton Trench. But we had to fight hand to hand to keep it. Ton Trench was rendered untenable by a shot covered by a Lewis gun.	
	8th.		The Batt. was reinforced by 2½ Coys. of the 11th W. Yorks. The Batt. was relieved by 2 Coys. of the 9th Yorks & 12 W. Yorks. 164 of W. Yorks remaining in, & proceeded to destr. Redoubt. The Batt. were relieved by the Camerons Highlanders & proceeded to Billets at Brule.	
	9th.		The Batt. rested.	
	10th.		The Batt. marched & entrained at Mericourt & detrained at Pont Remy & marched to Billets at Doudelainville.	
	11th.		The Batt. rested	
	12th.		The day was spent in inter-coy work.	
	13th.		The Batt. marched back to Pont Remy & entrained for Bailleul, & from there marched to Billets at a point 6 miles from Bailleul.	
	14th.		The Batt. waited, not having arrived at their Billets until 4.30 am between sorting & cleaning up.	
	15th 16th			
	17th.		The Batt. marched to billets in Area 16 near Steenwerck.	
	18th.		The Batt. marched to billets as follows:— H.Q. B.6.d.5.4 B.Coy B.6.c.6.3. C.Coy. C.1.d.3.2.1 D.Coy C.2.c.6.32. A Coy.	9405

WAR DIARY or INTELLIGENCE SUMMARY

Army Form C. 2118.

941 f
VB

Place	Date	Hour	Summary of Events and Information	Remarks and references to Appendices
	19th 20th 21st		Working parties of 300 men daily found for R.E.	
	22nd		The Batt. was relieved by the 9th Yorks. & 1 of our killed from the at CAPOT.	
	23rd 24th		The day was spent with Coy & Platoon training.	
	25th		The Batt. relieved the 9th Sherwood Foresters in trenches (Tr. 112½ / 122) Casualties: 2/Lt. P. Oatley killed. 1 OR wounded accidentally.	
	26th		Nothing of importance occurred. Casualties 1 OR killed. 5 OR wounded 2 Accidentally.	
	27th		— do — Casualties Nil.	
	28th		— do — Casualties Nil.	
	29th		Preparations were made to detonate gas against the enemy, but the weather was unpropitious, so nothing was done.	
	30th		The right gas was detonated against the enemy at 1.30 am. Our artillery started to bombard the enemy trenches at 1.34 am for 30 minutes. 2 Patrols from 9th went out to endeavour to enter enemy trenches & obtain identification but were unable to do so, owing to gas hanging about & enemy M.G. All returned safely. Casualties 5 Wounded.	
	31st		The day was quiet. The night enemy shelled the front line but did no damage. Casualties 2 OR wounded.	

M. Ustin Major
Commanding 8th Yorks. Regt.

WAR DIARY or INTELLIGENCE SUMMARY.

(Erase heading not required.)

8th Yorks

Army Form C.2118.

Place	Date	Hour	Summary of Events and Information	Remarks and references to Appendices
	1916. Sept. 1st.		Battalion relieved in the line by 9th. Yorks., we taking over from them. "A" & "B" Coys. HUNTERS AVENUE, "C" Coy TOUQUET FARM, "D" Coy PLOEGSTEERT WOOD. Casualties Nil.	
	2nd.		Day, quiet. That night gas was reported from front but after every one had "stood to" the alarm was cancelled. Casualty. 2/Lieut. H.R.B. Bailey bayonetted by sentry.	
	3rd.		Day quiet. Enemy aeroplane flew over Church parade very low but nothing happened. Casualties Nil.	
	4th.		Battalion was relieved by 7th. K.O.R. Lancashire Regt. and marched to camp at Anzac Training Area near Bailleul. Casualties Nil.	
	5th.		The day was spent in cleaning up.	
	6th.		Battalion entrained for ST. OMER, and marched to billets at HOULLE.	
	7th.		Company and platoon training carried out on Area "C" of Battalion Training Area.	
	8th. 9th.		Training in Area "D". The Battalion had the use of a range, and all companies fired including the Lewis Gunners. Bombing practice also carried out.	
	10th.		The day was spent in cleaning up and resting prior to the move to the Southern Area. The Battn. started at 10.55 p.m. from HOULLE, entraining at ST.OMER at 2 a.m.	
	11th.		Detrained at LONGUEAUX at 11.45 a.m. Marched through AMIENS to COISY and POULAINVILLE.	
	12th.		Starting at 8 a.m. the Battalion marched to HENENCOURT WOOD camp, reaching there at 3 p.m.	
	13th. 14th.		Platoon and Company training.	
	15th.		Whilst out on a Brigade Scheme the Battalion was recalled and marched to MILLENCOURT.	

WAR DIARY
or
INTELLIGENCE SUMMARY.
(Erase heading not required.)

Army Form C. 2118.

Place	Date	Hour	Summary of Events and Information	Remarks and references to Appendices
	16th.		Interior economy.	
	17th.		Cleaning up. Pte. Blunt was killed by a bomb accident.	
	18th.		Battalion marched from Millencourt to Reserve trenches near BAZENTIN-LE-PETIT WOOD taking over from 9th. Yorks.	
	19th.		"B" Coy. sent up to front line to support 9th. Yorks.	
	20th.		2 platoons of "B" Coy sent up for a similar purpose. Casualties. 2 men "B" Coy killed.	
	21st.		Remainder of Battalion engaged in carrying and working parties. Casualties. 2/Lieuts. BUSH and KILLACKY wounded.	
	22nd.		2/Lieuts. ROSS and HERON patrolled 1000 yards ahead of our front line. Received the thanks of the G.O.C. Relieved by 11th. Northumberland Fusiliers and marched to SCOTTS REDOUBT. Casualty 2/Lieut. Swain Killed.	
	23rd. 24th. 25th.		Battalion rested. Also supplied working parties daily.	
	26th.		The Battalion relieved the 9th. York & Lancs. in SHELTER WOOD.	
	27th. 28th. 29th. 30th.		Battalion in support. Resting and cleaning up. Large working parties daily. Casualties 1 O.R. wounded.	

W C Ruck Lieut. & Adj.
for Major
8th Yorkshire Regt.

Army Form C. 2118.

WAR DIARY
or
INTELLIGENCE SUMMARY.
(Erase heading not required.)

8 Yorks Rgt

Vol/13

12.2.
3 sheets

Instructions regarding War Diaries and Intelligence Summaries are contained in F.S. Regs., Part II. and the Staff Manual respectively. Title pages will be prepared in manuscript.

Place	Date	Hour	Summary of Events and Information	Remarks and references to Appendices
	1916. Oct. 1st.		The Battalion took over from the 9th. Battalion Yorkshire Regiment at the CUTTING, CONTALMAISON.	
	2nd.		The Battalion moved up to the line O.G. 1 & 2 to the right of the LE SARS Road, and took over from the 11th. Sherwood Foresters. A & D Coys. in O.G. 1 & 2; B Coy in trench behind DESTRIMONT trench; C Coy in ZIG ZAG trench.	
	3rd.		The enemy were comparatively quiet but enfiladed front trenches and caused casualties. The front trenches and communication trench in very bad condition.	
	4th.		The enemy shelled Headquarters dugout heavily with 5.9 and it had to be vacated. This evening a platoon of C Coy and Battalion Bombers attacked the trench and sap in O.G. 2, to the immediate right of the BAPAUME Road. The 10th. W.R. attacking O.G. 2 on the left of the road. Our attack succeeded but the latter failed. The position was consolidated and blocked. Three counter attacks were driven off by us.	
	5th.		Early this morning a fourth counter attack was driven off by us. There was considerable enemy shelling between 6 p.m. and 2 a.m. This night our heavy artillery shelled that portion of the trench captured by us on the 4th, killing 2 sgts. and several men, and we had to retire to our old position, which we handed over on relief to 9th. Yorks and Batt alion moved into support in PRUE, STARFISH, MARTIN ALLEY, and PUSH trenches. During this period in the trenches the weather was abominable, and communication, telephonic and otherwise, was very difficult. During this period the enemy artillery was very active. Our casualties for the period were - Killed. Off. Nil: O.R. 19. Wounded - Lieut. N.E.O. Story; 2/Lieuts. R.F. Wilson, A.W. Ross, A.P. Jackson, F. Ayton. O.R. 86: Wounded (Shell Shock) O.R. 5: missing O.R.1.	
	6th.		The Battalion found working parties to carry water, rations, and trench stores up to the front line.	
	7th.		The 68th. & 69th. Inf. Bdes. assaulted and captured LE SARS at 1.45 p.m. C Coy was sent up to reinforce the 9th. Yorks in LE SARS, and remained there until the 9th. Yorks were relieved.	

WAR DIARY
or
INTELLIGENCE SUMMARY.
(Erase heading not required.)

8th Yorkshire Regt

Army Form C. 2118.

28.
SB

Place	Date	Hour	Summary of Events and Information	Remarks and references to Appendices
	7th.		A heavy barrage was put on MARTINPUICH RIDGE during the attack, one of our orderlies being killed.	
	8th.		LE SARS was held and we provided working parties for carrying purposes as before. The 15th. Div. relieved the 23rd. Division on this day. The Battalion was relieved by the 7th. Cameron Highlanders and marched to SCOTS REDOUBT, arriving there about 10.30 p.m. Casualties during tour of trenches Oct. 2nd.- 8th:- Officers. Killed, Nil; Wounded 5. O.R. Killed, 29: Wounded, 121; Missing, 4: Shell shock, 6.	
	9th.		At 10 a.m. the Battalion marched to billets in ALBERT.	
	10th.		All the men bathed and were fitted out with new clothes.	
	11th.		The Corps Commander inspected and congratulated the 69th. Bde. on the work they have done, during their second visit to the Somme.	
	12th. 13th.		At 5 p.m. the Battalion entrained at ALBERT and proceeded to LONGPRE les CORPS SAINTES arriving where at 9.45 a.m. 13th. Motor buses met the train and conveyed the Battalion to billets at YVRENCHEUX.	
	14th.		Cleaning up and resting.	
	15th.		Marched to CONTEVILLE and entrained at 2.57 a.m. detraining at HOUPOU TRE at 9 a.m. Marched to billets in POPERINGHE.	
	16th to 22nd incl.		Parades each day. Working parties, guards and police were supplied for work in the Divl. Area. Received a draft of 90 O.R.	

Army Form C. 2118.

WAR DIARY
or
INTELLIGENCE SUMMARY.
(Erase heading not required.)

Instructions regarding War Diaries and Intelligence Summaries are contained in F. S. Regs., Part II. and the Staff Manual respectively. Title pages will be prepared in manuscript.

Place	Date	Hour	Summary of Events and Information	Remarks and references to Appendices
	23rd.		At 6 p.m. the Battalion entrained at POPERINGHE, detraining at YPRES at 8 p.m. Relieved the 11th. N.F. in the line, the same night. B & C Coys in the front line I.18.4 to I.24.4. D Coy in reserve in WELLINGTON CRESCENT, MAPLE COPSE and FORT ST. A Coy in RITZ TRENCH. Casualties Nil.	
	24th.		Usual trench life. The enemy were extremely quiet. Trenches were very wet and damaged. Work was begun at once.	
	25th.		Nothing unusual happened and the enemy were very quiet. Casualties Nil.	
	26th.		Wiring and work on the trenches carried on. C & D Coys. were relieved by A & B Coys respectively.	
	27th.		Nothing unusual happened. Enemy shelled MAPLE COPSE intermittently during the day.	
	28th.		Situation quiet. A good deal of wiring was done each night and the trenches were drained. Our snipers got much useful information during this tour of the trenches. Casualties. Nil.	
	29th.		On the night of the 29th. we were relieved by the 9th. Yorks, and took over their billets in the Infantry Barracks, YPRES.	
	30th 31st.		During the day the men rested and cleaned up. Each night working parties (250 strong) were sent to work in the front line in WARRINGTON AVENUE, GOUROCK ROAD, LOVERS LANE. Carrying parties provided.	

M Weatherhead
O.C. 8/ Yorkshire Regt.

29
213

Army Form C. 2118.

8th Yorkshire Regt.

Vol 14

13. 2.
3 sheets

WAR DIARY
or
INTELLIGENCE SUMMARY.
(Erase heading not required.)

Instructions regarding War Diaries and Intelligence Summaries are contained in F. S. Regs., Part II. and the Staff Manual respectively. Title pages will be prepared in manuscript.

Place	Date	Hour	Summary of Events and Information	Remarks and references to Appendices
NOVEMBER				
Offords	1st / 2nd		The Battalion still found the same working parties.	
	3rd		Usual Working Party.	
	4th		During the night of 4/5th the Battalion was relieved by the 9th Yorks & Lancs — continued at YPRES, bivouacked at BRANDHOEK and marched to TORONTO CAMP.	
Toronto Camp	5th/ 10th		The Battalion rested at Toronto Camp. Bathed at Poperinghe.	
	11th		On the night of the 10/11/16 the Battalion entrained at BRANDHOEK — detrained at YPRES, and relieved the 10th N.F.s on the right half of the right sector of the Division front. A,B & D Coys on the front line. C Coy in support on Stafford St. & Halifax St. During the day the enemy were very quiet. Casualties nil.	
Trenches	12th		Day quiet until 4 p.m. when the enemy bombarded CANADA TRENCH & St PIERRE St. for 1½ hours doing considerable damage. Our retaliation with T.M.B.s and artillery was good & stopped the enemy fire. Casualties killed 1 O.R. Wounded 2 O.R. lost 2 O.R.	
	13th		The day quiet. The enemy exploded a small camouflet at 3.40 pm opposite	

Army Form C. 2118.

WAR DIARY
or
INTELLIGENCE SUMMARY.
(Erase heading not required.)

Instructions regarding War Diaries and Intelligence Summaries are contained in F. S. Regs., Part II. and the Staff Manual respectively. Title pages will be prepared in manuscript.

Place	Date	Hour	Summary of Events and Information	Remarks and references to Appendices
	14th		Bdy. Patrol side occupied it. This together with enemy went on caps revealed the enemy's intentions in this sector little fire. Our aircraft was active. Wiring parties went out at night. Heavy T.M.B shelling by the enemy between 4.30 & 5.30 p.m. but day quiet otherwise. Our snipers much felt use of the excellent O.P. on this sector & obtained much important information.	
	15th		Day fairly quiet. Enemy T.M.Bs did not open. Our patrol investigated the enemy trench and found it reoccupied. Each night a wiring party worked at the gap. Usual sniping on both sides. Our sniper claim to have hit one German.	
	16th		Day was extremely quiet & that night we were relieved by the 9th Yorkshire Regt. We marched to billets at the Hospice Ypres. Total Casualties during this tour 1 killed 16 wounded	
YPRES.	17th {to 22nd}		The whole Battalion were out each day on working parties. On the 19th the Hospice was slightly shelled but we had no casualties. On the night of the 22/23rd we were relieved by the 9th York & Lancs and	

Army Form C. 2118.

WAR DIARY
or
INTELLIGENCE SUMMARY
(Erase heading not required.)

Instructions regarding War Diaries and Intelligence Summaries are contained in F. S. Regs., Part II. and the Staff Manual respectively. Title pages will be prepared in manuscript.

Place	Date	Hour	Summary of Events and Information	Remarks and references to Appendices
Toronto Camp	22nd 25th 29th		Battalion entrained for Toronto Camp. Working parties were supplied every other day & for rest on the Devizon area. Drill, Musketry exercises and wiring instruction was carried out each day by the Companies. On the night of the 28/29th the Battalion entrained at BRANDHOEK and detrained at YPRES and took over from the 11th N.F. in the right sector of the Divisional front. C & D Coys in front line I.18.3 to I.24.4. B & A Coys in support.	
	29th		Day quiet. Nothing to report.	
	30th		Usual hand bye. Both sides very quiet. Casualties Nil.	

A.M. Western
Lieut. Colonel.
Commanding 8th Yorkshire Regiment

War Diary

of

8th (Service) Battalion. A.P.W.O. Yorkshire Regiment.

1st December 1916.

to

31st December 1916.

Army Form C. 2118.

WAR DIARY
or
INTELLIGENCE SUMMARY.
(Erase heading not required.)

Instructions regarding War Diaries and Intelligence Summaries are contained in F. S. Regs., Part II. and the Staff Manual respectively. Title pages will be prepared in manuscript.

Place	Date	Hour	Summary of Events and Information	Remarks and references to Appendices
TRENCHES	1st.		A heavy mist hung between the lines the greater part of the day and much wire was put out.	
	2nd		CASUALTIES. a. M.P.D. was shot through the ankle carrying up rations. Day fairly quiet & nothing to report	
	3rd		Day passed quietly. At night the battalion was relieved by the 9th Yorks. and marched to billets at INFANTRY BARRACKS	
YPRES	4th			
	5th		Large working parties went out each night on working parties — Thickening parapet of WARRINGTON AV. etc.	
	6th			
	7th		This night we relieved the 9th Yorks & became the right Batt" on the left sector of the Div: front. A & B Coys on the front line. C & D Coys on support. Headquarters "TILE WORKS"	
Trenches	8th		Day fairly quiet until 1.15 pm to 3 pm. when enemy bombarded Batt" on the right with T.M's	
	9th		Quiet. nothing to report	
	10th		Usual enemy shelling at 12.30 pm	
	11th		Day quiet. This night the Batt" was relieved by 9th Yorks. & marched to billets at INFANTRY BARRACKS	
YPres.	12th			
	13th		Large working parties were found each day by the Batt". On the night of the 15th the Batt"	
	14th			
	15th		moved into Corps Reserve at TORONTO CAMP.	

Army Form C. 2118.

WAR DIARY
or
INTELLIGENCE SUMMARY.
(Erase heading not required.)

Instructions regarding War Diaries and Intelligence Summaries are contained in F.S. Regs., Part II. and the Staff Manual respectively. Title pages will be prepared in manuscript.

Place	Date	Hour	Summary of Events and Information	Remarks and references to Appendices
TORONTO CAMP	16th 17th 18th		Platoon Training. Working parties of 100 men were found.	
	19th		Platoon Training. Working party of 120 men was found. Cold weather. Snow fell in afternoon.	
	20th		Battn bathed in the morning at Poperinghe. Christmas Day celebrated. Dinners in camp. Very cold weather	
	21st 22nd		Platoon Training. Usual working parties.	
	23rd		Battn took over from the 13th D.L.I. & became left Battn in right sector of Divl front. A, B & D Coys in front line. B Coy in support. WINNIPEG ST. and the REDAN. Battn H/Q. DORMY HOUSE.	
TRENCHES	24th		Very Quiet - nothing to report.	
	25th		Quiet - normal artillery T.M. and machine gun fire.	
	26th		Usual movement in enemy lines was observed. Enemy aircraft flew low over our lines but returned when our machine guns opened fire.	
	27th		Day quiet, nothing to report. That night the Battn was relieved by 9th Yorks and took over then Billets in the BUND (ZILLEBEKE LAKE).	
BUND	28th 29th 30th		Fatigue working parties totalling 280 men were sent out each day to work on the front line. On the 30th the enemy slightly shelled the South end of the BUND	
	31st		At night we took over from the 9th Yorkshire Regt. in the same sector. O. on 232	

Army Form C. 2118.

8 Yorkshire Regt
Vol 16

152
8 shub

WAR DIARY
or
INTELLIGENCE SUMMARY.
(Erase heading not required.)

Place	Date	Hour	Summary of Events and Information	Remarks and references to Appendices
	January 1917			
Trenches	1st		Artillery on both sides active on this day. From 3 pm to 11pm the enemy subjected our trenches heavily with TMs and 77mm, at 5:30 pm our artillery bombarded enemy trenches on his left. The whole salient livened up. And the enemy suddenly thinking we were attacking opened up extremely heavy fire with TMs 4.2s and 77mm on our trenches for an hour. Trenches badly damaged – casualties 2 killed 9 wounded. 2/Lieut Barrowcliff wounded.	
	2nd		Much quieter. Both sides repairing damage caused by bombardments on the 1st inst.	
	3rd		Artillery fire increased. Enemy shelled our lines with TMs & shrapnel intermittently from 11am to 4 pm. Snipers on both sides active. Our Lewis Gunners successfully fired on enemy working party. Two bns relieved the P.O. went on a months leave and Major A.C.H Camke took command of the battalion.	
	4th		Day fairly quiet – usual artillery fire. This night we were relieved by the 2nd Yorkshire Regt and became Brigade Reserve in the BUND.	
BUND	5th		No working parties. The men rested. Hostile artillery fired on the BUND and YPRES.	
	6th		Working parties – 2/3 OR were found. Hostile artillery of the increased. YPRES was badly shelled.	
	7th		Working parties as before. The north end of the BUND was shelled heavily and artillery fire increased on YPRES. Casualties 1 OR wounded.	

Army Form C. 2118.

WAR DIARY
or
INTELLIGENCE SUMMARY.
(Erase heading not required.)

Instructions regarding War Diaries and Intelligence Summaries are contained in F. S. Regs., Part II. and the Staff Manual respectively. Title pages will be prepared in manuscript.

Place	Date	Hour	Summary of Events and Information	Remarks and references to Appendices
BUND	8th		The night the Battn was relieved by the 9th York & Lancs. Regt. The weather during the day of the BUND had been quite good	
	9th			
	10th		Thirteen N.C.O's were sent on local courses bops carried out a scheme of trenching and	
TORONTO	11th		N.C.O's 100 O.Rs were out each day on working parties. The weather was rather bad - rainy +	
CAMP	12th		cold. Reinforcements totalling 250 O.Rs arrived making the battalion up to full strength	
	13th		On the night of the 16/17th the battalion bivouaced at BRANDHOEK for YPRES and Toote	
	14th		over from the 10th N.Fs in the Infantry Barracks becoming Divisional Reserve.	
	15th			
	16th			
INFANTRY	17th		Much snow fell, trenching parties totalling 208 O.Rs were sent out	
BARRACKS	18th		As on the 17th. Nothing to report	
	19th		Nothing to report	
	20th		On the night of the 20th the battalion took over from the 9th Yorkshire Regt and became the left battalion on the left sector C & D Coys in the front line A & B Coys in support. Battalion Headquarters HALF WAY HOUSE	
TRENCHES	21st		Day fairly quiet - nothing much to report. The nights were very cold - often being 10° to 15° of frost	
	22nd		Nothing to report - still very cold	

Army Form C. 2118.

WAR DIARY
or
INTELLIGENCE SUMMARY.
(Erase heading not required.)

Instructions regarding War Diaries and Intelligence Summaries are contained in F.S. Regs, Part II and the Staff Manual respectively. Title pages will be prepared in manuscript.

Place	Date	Hour	Summary of Events and Information	Remarks and references to Appendices
TRENCHES	23rd		Artillery & aerial activity on both sides.	
	24th		The Battn was relieved by the 9th Yorkshire Regt and marched back to billets - INFANTRY BARRACKS	
INFANTRY	25th		YPRES, became Divisional reserve. Large working parties totalling 900 were sent out. Very cold.	
BARRACKS	26th		Nothing to report. Usual working parties. False gas alarm at night.	
	27th		Nothing to report	
	28th		This night the Battn relieved the 9th Yorkshire Regt & became the right battalion on Divl Front A - B Coy front line Hdqrs HALFWAY HOUSE.	
TRENCHES	29th		The day passed very quietly. The vicinity of Hdqs was shelled intermittently, but the front line trenches were quiet	
	30th		Nothing to report.	
	31st		At about 5.30 a.m. an S.O.S. rocket went up on our left. It was a raid by the enemy which was repulsed. Casualties during hour - 6 O.Rs.	

A.M. Fraser R.D.
Major
Commanding 8th Yorkshire Regt

Army Form C. 2118

WAR DIARY
or
INTELLIGENCE SUMMARY
(Erase heading not required.)

February 1917   6 York. Rgt   9th 17

Place	Date	Hour	Summary of Events and Information	Remarks and references to Appendices
IN THE FIELD.	1st		During the day the enemy shelled Headquarters a little with 4.2 shrapnel but did no damage. At night the Battalion was relieved by the 11th. Sherwood Foresters and marched back to quarters at TORONTO CAMP. Very severe frost.	
	2nd. to 8th.		During this period at Toronto Camp companies were enabled to carry out a successful scheme of training owing to the severe frost, which made the parade ground practicable for drill. Hours of work 9 a.m. to 3 p.m. The recruits showed a marked improvement at drill. Working parties averaging 75 strong were sent to YPRES each day. On the 6th. February the whole battalion bathed at the 23rd. Divisional Baths at POPERINGHE. Interesting inter-Coy. football matches were arranged each day, and on the night of the 8th. February a very successful Battalion concert was held in the Y.M.C.A. hut in camp. 2/Lieut. H.L.Oakley and 2/Lieut. G.M.Lister, original officers of the battalion reported for duty during the period, from England.	
	9th.		On the night of the 9th. C & D Coys and Headquarters left Toronto Camp and took over trenches from the 13th. D.L.I. becoming the right battalion on the Divisional Front. C, D Coys, a Coy of the 9th. Yorkshire Regiment holding the front line and battn. H.Q. at RUDKIN HOUSE. A & B Coys proceeded to the 69th. Brigade School for special training. During the relief the enemy bombarded our front with T.Ms. and field artillery. Fortunately no casualties and our artillery retaliated effectively.	
	10th.		Fairly quiet. During the morning the enemy shelled our left Coy. slightly, killing one Lewis Gunner and wounding four. Still very cold. At night our B Coy relieved the Coy. of the 9th. Yorkshire Regiment. A Coy. stayed at the 69th. Bde. School for four days training. The colonel returned from leave.	
	11th.		Quiet all day. A slight thaw set in.	
	12th.		Quiet until 2.30 p.m. when enemy sent over four or five T.Ms. killing one and wounding one. Thaw continues slowly. Two men wounded when out wiring.	
	13th.		The morning passed without event. During the afternoon from 2.30 p.m. to 4.30 p.m. the Corps Heavy Artillery bombarded the enemy's lines opposite our left and centre companies. At night the Battalion was relieved by the 9th. Yorkshire Regiment, and marched back to billets, Bn. H.Q. and B Coy. KRUISSTRAAT; A Coy. Cavalry Barracks, YPRES; C & D Coys the BUND. Total casualties 9th-13th. Feb. - Officers; Nil; O.Rs. 2 killed, 1 died of wounds, 10 wounded, 1 accidentally wounded.	

Army Form C. 2118

WAR DIARY
or
INTELLIGENCE SUMMARY

(Erase heading not required.)

Instructions regarding War Diaries and Intelligence Summaries are contained in F. S. Regs., Part II. and the Staff Manual respectively. Title Pages will be prepared in manuscript.

Place	Date	Hour	Summary of Events and Information	Remarks and references to Appendices
	13th.		Slight frost during the night.	
	14th.		The Battalion rested and cleaned up. Working parties (80 O.Rs.) were found for the Canadian Tunnelling Coy.	
	(15th. (16th.		Working parties (212 O.Rs) were found. These two days passed without event.	
	17th.		At night the Battalion relieved the 9th. Yorkshire Regiment in the trenches – Bn. H.Q. RUDKIN HOUSE; A, B & C Coys, front line; D Coy, support.	
	18th.		The day passed very quietly, and the night was unusually quiet. Our patrols were very active and found out much useful information about the enemy. Thaw still continues slowly.	
	19th.		Nothing to report and the night was very quiet.	
	20th.		At 3 a.m. a raiding party from the Battalion consisting of Lieut. F.C.Miller, and 28 O.Rs entered the enemy's trenches opposite our front. A Bangalore tube (ammonal) was used to cut a lane through the wire, and while the party was in the enemy's trenches the artillery maintained a box barrage. All arrangements worked excellently and the party entered the enemy's trenches without opposition. The Germans had evacuated their line and no prisoners were obtained. The party were in the enemy's trenches for half-an-hour and returned without suffering any casualty. The success of Commander of the Second Army and the G.O.C. 69th. Inf. Brigade complimented the party on the success of their arrangements. At 5 p.m. the Division on our left carried out a raid on a large scale. During the raid the enemy barraged our front line killing one man.	
	21st.		Day fairly quiet. At night the 9th. Yorkshire Regiment took over the trenches and the Battn. moved into Divisional reserve. Bn.H.Q. and B Coy, KRUISSTRAAT; A Coy, Cavalry Barracks, YPRES; C & D Coys, BUND.	
	22nd.		Usual working parties found.(212 O.Rs.) The Salient was very quiet.	
	23rd. 24th.			

1875 Wt. W593/826 1,000,000 4/15 J.B.C. & A. A.D.S.S./Forms/C.2118.

Army Form C. 2118

WAR DIARY
or
INTELLIGENCE SUMMARY
(Erase heading not required.)

Instructions regarding War Diaries and Intelligence Summaries are contained in F.S. Regs., Part II. and the Staff Manual respectively. Title Pages will be prepared in manuscript.

Place	Date	Hour	Summary of Events and Information	Remarks and references to Appendices
	23rd. 24th.		Nothing unusual happened. Major A.C.W.Cranko went into hospital and Capt. T.C.Mintoft assumed duties of Second in Command.	
	25th.		This night the Battalion was relieved by the 11th. Royal Sussex Regt, and marched to TORONTO CAMP.	
	26th.		The 23rd. Division was relieved by the 39th. Division, and the day was spent in fitting out ready for the march into Corps Rest.	
	27th.		At 9.40 a.m. the Battalion paraded and marched to billets at HOUTKERQUE. The Battalion marched excellently, no man falling out. Distance about 10 miles.	
	28th.		Starting at 8.45 a.m the Battalion marched to MILLAIN, a distance of 17 miles, arriving there at 4 p.m. Again the Battalion marched well.	

A.W. Western. Lieut Colonel.
Comdt. 8 Yorkshire Regt.

Vol 18

War Diary
of
8th (Service) Battalion. A.P.W.O. Yorkshire Regiment.

1st March 1917
to
31st March 1917.

Army Form C. 2118.

WAR DIARY
or
INTELLIGENCE SUMMARY.
(Erase heading not required.)

Instructions regarding War Diaries and Intelligence Summaries are contained in F.S. Regs., Part II. and the Staff Manual respectively. Title pages will be prepared in manuscript.

Place	Date	Hour	Summary of Events and Information	Remarks and references to Appendices
FIELD.	1st. March 1917.		Starting at 11.40 a.m. the Battalion marched from MILLAIN to billets at HOULLE, a distance of about 7 miles, arriving at 3.15 p.m.	
	2nd.		The day was spent in cleaning up and refitting. Weather - Mild.	
	3rd.		The Battalion marched to the training area. "A" & "B" Coys. fired on the rifle range, and "C" & "D" Coys. carried out platoon and Company training. The afternoon was spent in recreational training - inter-platoon football matches and cross-country running took place.	
	4th.		Church Parade in the morning and recreational training in the afternoon.	
	5th.		Physical training 7.30 a.m. to 8 a.m. Platoon Drill, Bayonet Fighting, and special classes - signallers, snipers, Lewis gunners and wiring were carried out in billets. Recreation. A fall of snow during the night which quickly disappeared during the day.	
	6th.		"A" & "B" Coys. fired on the range and "C" & "D" Coys. marched to the range training area - extended order drill and skirmishing. Recreation during the afternoon. Weather much brighter and mild.	
	7th.		The Battalion marched to the training ground, starting from billets at 8.30 a.m. and practised "THE ATTACK OF A VILLAGE". "D" Coy fired on "A" Range 2 p.m. - 5 p.m. Recreation. Weather - Very cold.	
	8th.		Parades in billets. Slight fall of snow.	
	9th.		As on the 8th. Weather still cold and slight fall of snow.	
	10th.		Parades in billets. "C" Coy on the range from 12 noon - 2 p.m.	
	11th.		Divine Service. Recreation.	
	12th.		Early morning parade. Skirmishing and deployment in Training Area. Rifle Range in afternoon. Special classes in bombing and wiring arranged each day.	
	13th.		Company route marches and rifle range. Boxing contests were arranged.	
	14th.		Battn. Exercise. (Attack Scheme) Recreation. Weather continues to be fine. Boxing contests took place.	

Army Form C. 2118.

WAR DIARY
or
INTELLIGENCE SUMMARY

(Erase heading not required.)

Instructions regarding War Diaries and Intelligence Summaries are contained in F.S. Regs., Part II. and the Staff Manual respectively. Title pages will be prepared in manuscript.

Place	Date	Hour	Summary of Events and Information	Remarks and references to Appendices
	15th.		Brigade Exercise. The Battalion carried out a practice attack.	
	16th.		Battalion rifle meeting - general training and recreational - inter-Coy. football matches.	
	17th.		The Battalion bathed at HOULLE Baths. Training in billets. "A" Coy. won the inter-Coy. football contest. Boxing at night.	
	18th.		Divine Service. Recreational training.	
	19th.		The Battalion paraded at 8.30 a.m. and marched to MILLAIN arriving there at 1 p.m.	
	20th.		Parading at 7.20 a.m. the Battalion marched to the HERZEELE Area (16 miles) arriving there at 1.30 p.m.	
	21st.		Marched to "Z" Camp. F.25.d.	
	22nd.		Training under Coy. arrangements. Special bombing, wiring and Lewis Gun classes were arranged.	
	23rd.		As for yesterday. The Battalion football team played the 9th. Yorkshire Regt. winning by 1 goal to Nil	
	24th.		Training as usual. Recreational training during the afternoon. Weather - fair.	
	25th.		Church Prades. The Colonel went on a course at the Second Army School and Capt. T.C.Mintoft took over command.	
	26th.		Parades as usual. Working party (50 O.Rs.) sent to PESELHOEK.	
	27th.		Parades.- Working party (60 O.Rs.) sent to SHELLHOEK.	
	28th.		The Army Commander inspected the Battalion. 180 men went to the Baths at GOUTHOVE.	
	29th.		Parades as usual. A working party (60 O.Rs.) sent to SHELLHOEK.	
	30th.		Nothing unusual to report. Working party (60 O.Rs.) sent to SHELLHOEK.	
	31st.		Training was carried out as usual. 90 men went to the baths at GOUTHOVE.	

M. Western. Lieut.Col.
Commdg. 8th. Yorkshire Regiment.

Army Form C. 2118

WAR DIARY
or
INTELLIGENCE SUMMARY
(Erase heading not required.)

6 Yorkshire Regt
Sept 19

182
2 sheets

Place	Date	Hour	Summary of Events and Information	Remarks and references to Appendices
	April 1917.			
	1st.		Church Parades. Recreation during afternoon. The Colonel returned and resumed Command.	
	2nd.		The G.O.C. Brigade inspected the Battalion.	
	3rd.		Usual Training. Two small working parties (20 men). A and B Cys.bathed at COUTHOVE.	
	4th.		Nothing to report. Working party (60 O.Rs.) was sent to SHELLHOEK. Weather fair but cold.	
	5th.		Nothing unusual to report. Company training.	
	6th.		Good Friday. Church parades. C and D Coy. bathed at COUTHOVE. Starting at 5 pm. the Battalion marched to TORONTO CAMP (G.18.a) - Transport Lines adjoining the Camp.	
	7th.		Usual Company training.	
	8th.		EASTER SUNDAY. Church parades. Recreation during the afternoon.	
	9th.		Nothing to report. Working party (60 O.Rs.) to PACIFIC SIDING.	
	10th.		Training. A and B Coys. bathed at WINNEPEG Camp. Working party (60 O.Rs.) to PACIFIC siding.	
	11th.		Training. Weather slight fall of snow. Cold North winds.	
	12th.		Early morning parades. Training by Companies. The rifle range was used.	
	13th.		As for yesterday.	
	14th.		During the day the Battalion cleaned up and rested. The Battalion entrained at BRANDHOEK at 9 pm.,detrained at Ypres and marched up to the trenches,taking over from the 9th.Y.O.Y.L.I. becoming the left battalion of the Brigade Front. Trenches I.30.9. to I.30.1.(the same trenches as handed over to the 9th.Yorkshire Regiment on Feb. 21st.).	
	15th.		A and D Coys. Front Line. B Coy. HALIFAX Area. C Coy. MAPLE St. Bn.H.Q. RUDKIN HOUSE. The trenches were in a bad state of repair and much salvage lay about - which necessitated large working parties. The day passed quietly. Casualties nil. The following casualties occurred to a working party of the Battn. attached to the R.E. 2/Lieut.A.G.Withington wounded. 1 O.R. killed. 7 O.Rs. wounded.	
	16th.		Nothing unusual happened. The enemy sent over a few rifle grenades and a few shells fell on Maple St. During all hours of darkness patrols of our Battn. wereout. Weather rainy. Casualties 1 O.R. accidentally self inflicted.	
	17th.		Very quiet. Weather much brighter no rain.	
	18th.		Nothing to report. Slight fall of snow. The Battalion was relieved by the 9th.Yorkshire Regt. and took over their billets becoming Bde.Support Battn. B.C.D. Coys. in BUND. Headquarters and A Coy. in RAILWAY DUGOUTS.	

Army Form C. 2118

WAR DIARY
or
INTELLIGENCE SUMMARY

(Erase heading not required.)

Instructions regarding War Diaries and Intelligence Summaries are contained in F.S. Regs., Part II. and the Staff Manual respectively. Title Pages will be prepared in manuscript.

Place	Date	Hour	Summary of Events and Information	Remarks and references to Appendices
	19th. 20th. 21st.		Working Parties, totalling 3 Officers and 230 O.Rs. were sent out each day. Work consisted chiefly of carrying stores up to the Front line at night. The Salient was very quiet - little shelling during this tour. Weather fair.	
	22nd. to 29th.		Battalion in TORONTO Camp. Usual Training. Bayonet Fighting and Obstacle Courses constructed. During night of 28/29th. sudden orders to march to STEENVORDE Area.	
	29th. 30th.		Arrived at STEENVORDE and billeted in scattered farms outside the village. Usual inspection and cleaning up. Making up deficiencies etc. Magnificent weather.	

W. Western   Lieut. Colonel

Commanding 8th. Yorkshire Regiment.

Army Form C. 2118.

WAR DIARY

or

~~INTELLIGENCE SUMMARY~~

(Erase heading not required.)

Instructions regarding War Diaries and Intelligence Summaries are contained in F. S. Regs., Part II. and the Staff Manual respectively. Title pages will be prepared in manuscript.

Place	Date	Hour	Summary of Events and Information	Remarks and references to Appendices
FIELD.	1917 1.May.		Battalion Parade. Inspection and drill. Recreational Training in the afternoon.	
	2nd.		Battalion inspected with 9th. Yorkshires by General Sir JAMES BABINGTON, K.C.M.G. and complimented on their smart turnout and appearance. 2/Lieut. C.W.Jones decorated with Military Cross for gallantry.	
	3rd.		Battalion exercise. A & B Coys. under Capt. PEARSON attacked C & D Coys. under Major Cranko. Several officers visited Second Army Bomb School at TERDEGHEM.	
	4th.		Parades in billets. Brigade Signalling Scheme. Recreational Training. Football - A v.D Coy. B v. C Coy. Perfect summer weather. Lieut. J.T.Shaw, Lieut. A.G.McCulloch and 2/Lt. J.L.Armstrong reported for duty.	
	5th.		Marched to HEKSKEN, M.3.c.2.2. in the BOESCHEPE area starting at 5.30 a.m. Arriving about 10 a.m. pitched camp in field, some of the officers being billeted in WESTOUTRE.	
	6th.		Supplied large parties for work under Xth. Corps R.E. Practically whole battalion employed in shifts from 4 a.m.- 8 a.m.; 8 a.m. - 12 noon, and noon till 4 p.m., 4p.m. - 8 p.m. unloading heavy shells and stores and working on dumps at HEKSKEN, RENINGHELST and ATLANTIC SOUTH sidings.	
	7th.		Major Mintoft left for 10 days leave to Paris.	
	8th.		Lieut. A.W.Ross and 2/Lieut. P.J.Killacky rejoined for duty from England.	
	9th.		Half Battalion marched in the morning to the BOESCHEPE Area for training. The bombers under Lieut. Lister did special training.	
	10th.		Working parties as before. Large part of the Battalion had baths.	
	11th.		Same as 10th. Entertained two Belgian artillery officers at Headquarters.	
	12th.		A competition between coys. transport was won by "A" Coy. Highly satisfactory. Major Cranko left the battalion for new appointment. During our stay at HEKSKEN the C.O. continued his equitation class for officers which was begun at STEENVOORDE.	

Army Form C. 2118.

WAR DIARY
or
INTELLIGENCE SUMMARY.
(Erase heading not required.)

Instructions regarding War Diaries and Intelligence Summaries are contained in F.S. Regs., Part II. and the Staff Manual respectively. Title pages will be prepared in manuscript.

Place	Date	Hour	Summary of Events and Information	Remarks and references to Appendices
	13th.		Struck camp early and marched by Coys. to WINNEPEG. Transport at HALIFAX. After resting, the Battalion marched to the BUND (2 Coys), "B" & "D" marching to Promenade dugouts, YPRES. 2/Lieut. Gregory and platoon from "D" Coy reported to 101st. Coy R.E. for working parties. 2/Lieut. Gregory killed by a shell in Ypres whilst getting his men out of the baths.	
	14th.		C.O. left the Bund for short leave, Capt. R.C.Grellet taking over command. Each Coy. provided working parties of 120 strong each evening under 101 and 102 Coys. R.E. Sgt. Dwyer and 1 O.R. died of wounds received in the morning at the Bund.	
	15th.		Working parties as before at night.	
	16th.		B. & D. Coys. relieved A & C Coys. in the Bund, the latter marching back to HALIFAX CAMP after working in the early morning.	
	17th.		A & C Coys. sent 120 men each night by lorries to work in the line. B. & D Coys. continued as previous nights. Major Mintoft returned from Paris and took over temporary command.	
	18th.		On the night/the Battalion moved to Hill 60 sub-sector, and took over trenches from 12th. D.L.I. of the 18/19th.	
	19th.		Day fairly quiet. Our artillery busy cutting wire.	
	20th.		Nothing further to report. Wire cutting still proceeded. Hostile artillery not active. Two men slightly wounded.	
	21st.		Nothing unusual happened. Large parties were found each night to carry bombs and rations to the dumps.	
	22nd.		At 3 a.m. a raiding party consisting of Lieut. Hiley and 20 O.Rs. of "B" Coy attempted to surprise an enemy advanced post, but unfortunately a S.O.S. was sent up from the battalion on our right and the consequent shelling and dawn made the raid impossible. Wire cutting by our artillery and usual carrying parties.	
	23rd.		Nothing unusual to report.	
	24th.		The day passed fairly quietly.	

Army Form C. 2118

WAR DIARY
or
INTELLIGENCE SUMMARY
(Erase heading not required.)

Place	Date	Hour	Summary of Events and Information	Remarks and references to Appendices
	25th.		At 2.a.m. 24th/25th. the Battalion was relieved by the 11th. Sherwood Foresters, marched to Brandhoek and entrained for ABEELE. The Battalion arrived in billets 2 miles N.W. of Abeele (K.23.d.) at 9 a.m. and rested during the remainder of the day. The Colonel returned from leave and assumed command.	
	26th.		Officers and a proportion of N.C.Os. visited the practice trenches at WATON FRANCE. The remainder of the battalion spent the day in cleaning up, inspections and interior economy.	
	27th.		A Brigade Church Parade under Brigadier General LAMBERT was held at B Coys. billets. After parade the officers and N.C.Os. visited the practice trenches.	
	28th.		Parades under Coy. arrangements. Coys. practised attack formations, bayonet fighting, drill etc. A model of the trenches was finished in plaster, by Lieut OAKLEY.	
	29th.		During the morning the Battalion practised the attack over the practice trenches. Then the Brigade rehearsed the same attack. Dinner was taken. Weather very hot. 2/Lt. Wheeler reported for duty.	
	30th.		The whole Brigade again rehearsed the attack. Dinner out. Weather splendid.	
	31st.		During the morning the battalion attacked over the practice trenches. Dinner out. Carried out wood fighting in BEAUVOORDE WOOD. A successful battalion concert was held at 7 p.m. under the auspices of the Padre. Rev. Williams. The concert was made an occasion for presenting the Colonel with a souvenir of his wedding. Orders to move to SCOTTISH LINES were received at 10.30 p.m.	

CM Western Lieut.Colonel,

Commanding 8th. Yorkshire Regiment,

WAR DIARY
or
INTELLIGENCE SUMMARY

Army Form C. 2118

(Erase heading not required.)

6/2/3 4th Yorkshire Regt.

Place	Date	Hour	Summary of Events and Information	Remarks and references to Appendices
	June 1st. 2nd.		Moved to Scottish Lines in the OUDERDOM Area. A long and trying march. Weather very hot. Took over huts with Transport bivouaced near.	
	3rd. 4th.		Usual parades. Practice in making hasty wire entanglements and practice in wire cutting. Battalion bathed at Poperinghe Baths. Brigade concentrated in OUDERDOM area. Weather excellent. Brigade Church parade. Usual parades. Issue of assaulting material such as bombs, sandbags, extra wire cutters etc. Yukon Pack compeition in afternoon. Won by 9th.Yorkshire Regt. 8th.Yorkshire Regt.second.	
	5th.		Preparations for proceeding to the trenches. Corps-Commander General Sir H.L.MORLAND held a conference with Battalion Commanders. Left for trenches at 8.30 pm. via TORONTO Camp passing 2nd.Battn.Yorkshire Regt. en route. Special Report.	
	5th. to 12th.		The Battalion left SCOTTISH LINES on the night of 5/6 June and marched up to the trenches. Hostile shelling heavy in some places with intermittent bursts of lachrymatory and gas shell. Gas Helmets were worn. Eleven casualties from shell fire. Headquarters B D and C Coy. (less two platoons) went to LARCH WOOD TUNNELs. A Coy. and 2 platoons C Coy. to S.P. 9. The 6th.June was uneventful. Assembly trenches were inspected; platoons "told off" for certain exits in the tunnels. Everyone rested as far as possible. At 2 am. 7th.June A Coy. and two platoons of C Coy. had adavanced to PANAMA CANAL and JACKSON AVENUE; and at 2.30 am. the battalion were reported to be in their assembly trenches, and were inspected by the Commanding Officer. All were in excellent spirits. Shelling on both sides died away to nothing. Enemy continuously sent up Very Lights from Hill 60. At 3 am. the men got out of the assembly trenches and lay down in front of them. At 3.10 am. the ground shook and trembled. Both mines exploded and our guns opened fire. Advance was difficult owing to the darkness, but a steady advance was maintained. A and B Companies had made allowances for the lips of craters being more extensive and accordingly made unnecessarily large detours. This however they remedied on reaching the high ground. Both Captain Lambert M.C. and Captain B.L.Pearson M.C. handled their companies with great skill and gallantry. They broadened their front, changed direction half right and half left respectively, and captured the RED objective with great dash. Meanwhile C Coy. under Capt. R.G.Atkinson had been advanced direct on the two mine craters. Enemy resistance was at once overcome and consolidation was commenced at 3.20 am. Battalion Headquarters had started in front of the leading wave; but on reaching DEEP SUPPORT were so far in front of the Battalion that a halt had to be made. They pushed on again at	

Army Form C. 2118.

WAR DIARY
or
INTELLIGENCE SUMMARY.
(Erase heading not required.)

Instructions regarding War Diaries and Intelligence Summaries are contained in F. S. Regs., Part II. and the Staff Manual respectively. Title pages will be prepared in manuscript.

Place	Date	Hour	Summary of Events and Information	Remarks and references to Appendices
			3.20 am. and by 3.30 am. were established on the Eastern slope of HILL 60 at the MOUND according to instructions received from Brigade. The Signallers had followed the fourth wave, laying a wire as they advanced. In the meantime A and B Coys.with hardly a check on the RED Line had pushed on to the BLUE objective; close to our own barrage. Both Coys. advanced a little beyond the BLUE Line which fault I attribute to the fact that the enemy ran from shell holes near the objective, and men could not be restrained from pursuit. Also the hostile trenches had been so destroyed that it was difficult to verify one's position. Both coys. pushed out patrols according to orders; but these were these beyond our own barrage for 5 hours. At 3 hours 40 minutes after Zero "D" Coy. passed through in artillery formation and occupied the BLACK Line with hardly a casualty and meeting practically no resistance. As, however, the troops on their left and right had not advanced quite so far and also "D" Coys. orders were to link up to these two Battalions, they accordingly withdrew and immediately got in touch with both flanks. The morning was spent in reorganising in depth, consolidating and putting strong points in a state of defence, carrying up material,stores etc. "A" Coy. were relieved on the night 10/11th.June and wentinto reserve in the copses near ZILLEBEKE. Battalion less a Coy. was relieved on the night 11/12 June. Night of 12/13 June, Battalion moved to MONTREAL CAMP in lorries. The preparations for the attack were all that could be desired. The artillery preparation was successful beyond one's wildest hopes. Assembly trenches and arrangements for evacuating the tunnels were excellent. Supplies, material etc. were very ably organised. CASUALTIES. Captain E.N.Lambert and 2/Lieut. W.Buckle Died of Wounds 7.6.17. Captain B.L.Pearson, Lieut.A.G. McCullock, 2/Lieut.C.W.Jones 2/Lieut.J.L.Armstrong, Lieut.J.T. Shaw, 2/Lieut.W.H.Mitchell Wounded 7.6.17. 2/Lieut.H.J.Smith and 2/Lieut.A.T.Dudley Wounded at Duty 9.6.17. Other Ranks. Killed in Action and Died of Wounds 35. Missing 13. Wounded 191. Wounded at duty 4. Missing believed Killed 1. Missing believed Wounded 1.	
	13th.		Stayed in Montreal Camp until 4.30 pm. Men very tired but in good spirits. Marched to BERTHEN area. A and C Coys. billeted in barns, B and D Coys. tents arrived about 8.30 pm. Lieut. W.E. Bush roceded on leave. 2/Lieut.H.L.Oakley assumed duties of Adjt.	
	14th.		Day spent in resting and cleaning up. Glorious weather.	
	15th.		Cleaning up, Inspection and making up deficiencies.	

WAR DIARY or INTELLIGENCE SUMMARY

(Erase heading not required.)

Army Form C. 2118

8 Yorkshire Rgt

Place	Date	Hour	Summary of Events and Information	Remarks and references to Appendices
	16th.		Battalion bathed. Usual parades.	
	17th.		Brigade Church parade. The Battalion was afterwards inspected by Major Gen. Sir. J.M.Babington K.C.M.G. Commanding the Division. and was congratulated by him on the fine work and successful operations of June 7th. Lt. WILLIAMS East Lancs.Regt.joined for duty and posted to B Coy.	
	18th.		Usual parades. Special training commenced for Lewis Gunners and other specialists.	
	19th.		Battalion Training. Gas Helmets inspected by Divisional Gas Officer. Brigade Horse show in afternoon. The Battalion took 2nd.place in the water cart and Lewis Gun Limber Competitions. Lieut.Col. Western and Capt. Atkinson were 1st. and 2nd. in the Officers Hurdly race.	
	20th.		B and C Coys. under Capt.Atkinson proceed in motor lorries to DICKEBUSH for road construction work. Usual parade for A and D Coys. A team composed of Officers and men played the 11th. West Yorks.Regt. at cricket. Defeated by 20 runs.	
	21st.		A Coy. carried out Musketry practiceon 9th.Corps.Range. D Coy. usual parades and wiring. Special class for N.C.Os. commenced under the R.S.M. Weather changed to frequent showers.	
	22nd.		A and D Coys. carried out training under Coy.arrangements. N.C.Os under R.S.M.	
	23rd.		As for yesterday. 2/Lieut.C.T.Hepworth 12th.Lancers. and 2/Lieut.G.F.Pearce 9th.Lancers joined the Battalion and were posted to A and D Coys.	
	24th.		Brigade Church parade.	
	25th.		A and D Coys. carried out training – Musketry, Arms drill, squad drill etc. /Lt E Bush returned from top	
	26th.		9th.Corps Rifle Rangewas allotted to D Coy. for musketry practice.	
	27th.		Range again allotted to A and D Coys.	
	28th.		During the day the Battalion less B and C Coys. rested preparatory to the move to the CHIPPEWA area.At 4 pm. the Battalion started from billets (H.l.d.) in BERTHEN area and marched via GODEWAERSVELDE to ALBERTA Camp one mile south of REMINGHELST, arriving there at 9 pm. The Battalion marched excellently. B and C Coy.joined the Battalion in ALBERTA Camp on arrival. Advance parties proceeded to the trenches (Hill 60 Sector). During the night much rain fell.	
	29th.		The morning was spent in inspections and preparations for the trenches. Eight new Officers arrived (first appointment) 2/Lieut.R.R.Crute, J.H.McNicholas, L.C.Dickens, Wm.Lister, F.C.Vernon, C.A.Bottomley, E.Clegg, J.H.Morrison, J.Mills. At 4.30 pm. the Battalion left Campand marched via DICKEBUSH to the trenches. A Halt was made for an hour for teas at DICKEBUSH. Relief was completed by 2.30 am. and although the Battalion was shelled en route, only 2 men were wounded. The line held was slightly in advance of the position the battalion assaulted and captured on 7th.inst. The line consisted of a series of posts and the position of the enemy could not accuratelybe determined.A considerable amount of rain fell during the day making the trenches extremely wet.	
	30th.			

for Lieut.Colonel
Commanding 8th.Yorkshire Regiment.

WAR DIARY
or
INTELLIGENCE SUMMARY.

(Erase heading not required.)

Army Form C. 2118.

Place	Date	Hour	Summary of Events and Information	Remarks and references to Appendices
	July 1917. 1st.		Fairly quiet day. Weather held fine. The battalion was relieved by the 10th. West Riding Regt. and became Reserve Battalion. Battn.H.Q. at LARCH WOOD. IMMOVABLE Support and WINDY CORNER. C Coy. LARCH WOOD. D Coy. S.P.9. A and D Coys.	
	2nd. 3rd.		The battalion rested during the day and supplied large working parties at night. The day passed quietly. At night the battalion was relieved by a battalion of the 47th. Division and marched back to MICMAC CAMP.	
	4th.		At 4 a.m.whilst the Battalion was bivouacing in MICMAC Camp an enemy aeroplane flew over at a low altitude and dropped two bombs. One man was killed. Leaving camp at 11.30 am. the battalion marched to OUDERDOM and entrained for GODWAERSVELDE. The march was then continued to billets 2 miles north of STEENVOORDE. Transport moved by road from MICMAC Camp. Weather - Very hot.	
	5th. 6th.		The day was spent in cleaning up, making up deficiencies etc. Parades under Coy.arrangements,reorganising platoons, sections etc. A draft of 219 O.Rs. arrived. 50% of the draft had not been on active service before. The whole Battalion bathed at STEENVOORDE Divn.Baths.	
	7th.		A programme of training was drawn up by the Commanding Officer for the ensuing week. As training ground was limited the training was done by coys. 7 - 7.30 am. Physical Training. 9 am. to 12 noon - Arms drill, Bayonet Fighting, Musketry, Coy. drill etc. The "Platoon Attack" was practised each day. The afternoons were devoted to recreational training - Cricket. The Divisional Commander Major General Sir J.M.Babington K.C.M.G. inspected the draft of 219 O.Rs. which arrived on 6th.inst, and presented medal ribbons to the undermentioned-	

Military Medals.

No.11630 Sergt.J.Walker.	No.19313 Cpl.R.Jackson.	No.13080 L.Cpl.C.Nichols.
No.14893 Sergt.J.Griffiths.	No.14312 Cpl.T.W.Hewison.	No.11959 L.Cpl.J.A.Duffy.
No.14614 Sergt.F.S.Cooper.	No.12110 Cpl.T.Williams.	No.13090 Pte. R.Akers.
No.13899 Sergt.W.Bottoms.	No.15755 Cpl.J.Willson.	No.15560 Pte. J.Day.
No.14269 Sergt.J.Stinson.	No.19397 Cpl.R.Waters.	No.11289 Pte. W.Thompson.
No.21811 Pte. C.D.Saul.	No.13940 Cpl.R.Turnbull.	No.13108 Pte. E.Armstrong.
No.13489 Cpl. G.Clark.	No.12838 Cpl.T.Carroll.	No.23346 Pte. J.W.Wells.
No.12898 Cpl. E.Boyle.	No.13983 L.C.T.Keogan.	14244 Pte. J.Hanlon.
	No.33132 Pte.J.Smith.	

| | 8th. 9th. | | On account of the inclement weather Church Parade was cancelled. A new class of N.C.Os commenced under the R.S.M. A draft of 64 O.Rs. arrived. Usual parades and recreational training. The Brigade Commander inspected the new draft of 64 O.Rs. | |

WAR DIARY

or

INTELLIGENCE SUMMARY

(Erase heading not required.)

Army Form C. 2118

Place	Date	Hour	Summary of Events and Information	Remarks and references to Appendices
	10th.		Usual parades. Weather hot. Major General Sir J.M.Babington K.C.M.G. presented medal ribbons to the undermentioned - Military Cross. 2/Lieut.A.T.Dudley. Lieut.J.P.Reed. 2/Lieut.J.P.Heron. D.C.M. No.14770 C.S.M. W.Masheder. No.11577 Sergt.A.Knowles. No.11751 Pte.A.Smith. D.S.O. Capt.B.L.Pearson M.C. (not present.Wounded in hospital in England)	
	11th.		A Bullet and Bayonet Course was erected. Leaving billets at 10 am. the battalion marched via STEENVOORDE to GODSWAERSVELDE entraining at 2 pm.- detrained at OUDERDOM and marched to MICMAC Camp. The same C and D Coys.proceeded to the line in motor lorries and took over from 2Nth.support coys. of the 68th.Inf.Brigade.	
	12th.		The remainder of the battalion bivouaced in MICMAC Camp during the day and proceeded to the line by march route, Commencing 7.45 pm. The battalion took over from 12th.D.L.I. and became right battalion front line. Disposition :- C and D Coys. Front Line. A and B Coys. Support. Bn.H.Q. IMP support.	
	13th.		The relief was completed without casualties. Active Artillery on both sides fairly active. During the afternoon and night much rain fell and the trenches became almost impassible. The front line consisted of a continuous trench with a few outlying posts. At dusk and dawn the enemy always put down a practice barrage - shells of all calibres including gas shells.	
	14th.		Weather brightened up considerably and observation was good. Increased activities on both sides - artillery and aircraft. Throughout the day and part of the night the enemy bombarded our left coy. (D) causing 30.casualties (5 Killed) 2/Lieut.Mills and 2/Lieut.Morrison were also wounded. Our artillery retaliated.	
	15th.		Weather still good. Our artillery fire increased. The right Coy H.Q. (C) was shelled but only one man was killed - none wounded.	
	16th.		Normal activity. The battalion was relieved this night by the 11th.West Yorkshire Regt.and became reserve battalion.	
	17th. 19th)		Whilst reserve battalion large working parties were found each night - carrying up ammunition rations etc. to form dumps for the coming advance. On the night 19th.inst.the battalion took over from the 11th.West Yorkshire Regt.- A & B Coys. Front Line. C & D Coys. Support.	
	20th.		Normal activities. The support Coys. found working parties each night.	

WAR DIARY
or
INTELLIGENCE SUMMARY

(Erase heading not required.)

Army Form C. 2118

Instructions regarding War Diaries and Intelligence Summaries are contained in F.S. Regs., Part II. and the Staff Manual respectively. Title Pages will be prepared in manuscript.

Place	Date	Hour	Summary of Events and Information	Remarks and references to Appendices
	21st.		Nothing unusual happened. The enemy put down very heavy barrages on our communication trenches each day at dusk and dawn. C and D Coys. were relieved by the 9th.E.Surreys and marched back to MICMAC Camp.	
	22nd.		Our artillery fire increased. During this period the front line was very seldom shelled by the enemy. A and B Coys. sustained no casualties. At night Battn.H.Q., A and B Coys. were relieved by the 9th.East Surrey Regt. and marched back to MICMAC Camp. During this period the Regtl.Transport experienced great difficulty in bringing rations up. Pack mules by daylight were used on several occasions. Part of the Regtl.Transport was also used for bringing up ammunition for the coming offensive. Casualties to the Transport 2 O.Rs. wounded and 1 mule killed.	
	23rd.		The Brigade moved to the BERTHEN area. Marching out from MICMAC Camp at 3 pm. the battalion proceeded via LA CLYTTE - WESTHUTRE to BERTHEN Area arriving in billets at 9 pm.	
	24th.		The day was spent in cleaning up,inspecting and reorganising. Brigadier General T.S.Lambert inspected all the new drafts which had arrived since June 7th. (total 330 O.Rs). Weather fair.	
	25th.		Major General Sir J.M.Babington K.C.M.G. inspected the battalion at 10.30 am. He also presented medal ribbons to - Military Cross. 2/Lieut. J.T.Lakin. Military Medals. No.14827 Pte. H. Guy. No.18332 Pte. J. Wood. No.18609 Pte. H. Dresser. No.13388 Pte. S. Watson. who were not presented at the previous parades. Weather rainy.	
	26th.		The Brigade moved to the BOISDINGHEM Area. Leaving billets at 10 am. the battalion marched via FLETRE to CAESTRE where it entrained for ST.OMER. Arrived at ST.OMER 6 pm. marched via ST.MARTINS - TATINGHEM - QUELMES to billets in ACQUIN arrived at 11 pm.	
	27th. 28th. 29th.		Day spent in cleaning up, reorganising and resting. Billets very good - weather very hot. 7 - 7.30 am. Physical Training. 9 to 12.30 pm. Parades-under Coy. arrangements. Inspection by O.C. Coys. Church parades. Recreational Training. Refresher Class for Sergts. commenced under R.S.M.	
	30th.		The range at Q.29.c.was allotted to the battalion for the whole day,but on account of the heavy rain could not be used. Training confined to billets. A Battalion Plunge bath was erected in a stream at ACQUIN and the battalion was bathed in it.	
	31st.		"A" Range at Q.14.b.was allotted as follows - A & B Coys.8.30 am.- 1.30pm. C & D Coys.2.30 pm.- 6 pm. Weather - still rainy.	

M. Weston.
Lieut-Colonel
Commanding 8th. Yorkshire Regiment.

Vol 23

Howard
5 shut

War Diary
of
8th (Service) Battalion. A.P.W.O. Yorkshire Regiment.

1st. August 1917.
to.
31st. August 1917.

Army Form C. 2118.

WAR DIARY
or
INTELLIGENCE SUMMARY.

(Erase heading not required.)

Instructions regarding War Diaries and Intelligence Summaries are contained in F. S. Regs., Part II. and the Staff Manual respectively. Title pages will be prepared in manuscript.

Place	Date	Hour	Summary of Events and Information	Remarks and references to Appendices
IN THE FIELD.	1917. Aug. 1.		The whole Battalion fired on "A" Range. Refresher course for Sergeants, under R.S.M.	
	2nd.		A 60 yards Lewis Gun range and a 100 yards rifle range were constructed near the billets. Three companies marched to the area and carried out field training. One Coy. remained in billets and used the ranges. Heavy showers during the day.	
	3rd.		Rained continuously throughout the day. Battn. remained in billets. Musketry, lectures etc.	
	4th.		Training again confined to billets on account of the rain.	
	5th.		Divine Service. All Lewis Guns were fired on the Battn. range.	
	6th.		The Battn. less B Coy. marched out of billets at 8.30 a.m. to No.1. Southern area, and carried out training. B Coy. were allotted the Battn. ranges. Sgt. Moore, Instructor for P. & B.T. attached to the Battn. and commenced class for 4 Officers and 8 N.C.Os.	
	7th.		The Battn. assembled on a training area near billets and was inspected while at work by Gen. Sir H.C.O. Plumer, G.C.M.G. G.C.V.O., K.C.B. A.D.C. Today is the anniversary of Lieut.Col. B.C.M.Western, D.S.O. taking over command of the Battalion.	
	8th.		A.B.C.Coys. Training area. D Coy. Battn. Ranges. During the afternoon Bn. Athletic Sports were held with great success.	
	9th.		Moved by march route at 1 p.m. to HOULLE. Billets rather crowded. The Division was transferred to the Fifth Army. XVIII Corps. Sgt. Moore's class finished.	
	10th.		Parades under Coy. arrangements near billets. A 50 yards rifle range and a 60 yards Lewis Gun range were renovated at W.10 and used throughout the day. Lecture to C.O. and Coy. Commanders by Corps Gas Officer.	
	11th.		Battalion carried out the usual training on the allotted area. Lieut.Gen. Sir IVOR MAXSE, XVIII Corps Commander addressed the senior officers of the Battalion in the school at HOULLE.	

Army Form C. 2118.

WAR DIARY
or
INTELLIGENCE SUMMARY.
(Erase heading not required.)

Instructions regarding War Diaries and Intelligence Summaries are contained in F.S. Regs., Part II. and the Staff Manual respectively. Title pages will be prepared in manuscript.

Place	Date	Hour	Summary of Events and Information	Remarks and references to Appendices
	12th.		Brigade Church Parade in the Regimental Transport Field. No. 12529 Pte. CLEMINSON J. and No. 41589 Pte. S.HOOKER were presented with the Military Medal Ribbon by Brig. Gen. T.S.Lambert. Reinforcement of 12 O.Rs. Weather fair.	
	13th.		Baths at HOULLE for the whole battalion. Coy. training under O.C.Coys. Intensive digging, platoon attacks etc. Scheme for officers and sergeants under 2nd. in Command. D Coy. night patrol work.	
	14th.		All Coys. fired on ranges at Q.10. Other work - rapid deployment, intensive digging, platoon attacks on the training area. B Coy. night patrol work. Weather hot.	
	15th.		All coys. on No.1 Northern Training areas. A four days course at the XVIII Corps Special School commenced. O.C.Coys. and one other officer per Coy. attended.	
	16th.		A & C Coys. Battn. snipers and signallers carried out the usual training on the area. B & D Coys. were allotted the bullet and bayonet course at K.36. "B" Range was used by all coys. during the afternoon. A reinforcement of 34 O.Rs. arrived. 2/Lt. Morrison rejoined the Battn.	
	17th.		Whole Battalion on No.2. Southern area - platoon attacks, drill, ceremonial etc. Night operations. -All Coys. practised forming up on tapes for an attack. Reinforcement of 37 O.Rs. arrived.	
	18th.		Range at Q.10 allotted to Coys. Other parades under Coy. arrangements. The officers who proceeded on course at XVIII Corps School returned.	
	19th.		The Battalion carried out a field firing practice at GUEMY. 7.30 a.m. - 4 p.m.	
	20th.		Battalion on No.1. Northern Training area - Usual parades. Personnel of Hdqrs. Q.M.Stores and Transport bathed at the Divisional baths at HOULLE. Night operations. The Brigade practised forming up on tapes for an attack. 8.30 - 11 p.m. 2/Lt. F.Robinson and 2/Lt. T.E.Hardcastle joined the Battalion.	
	21st.		Brigade attack scheme in the Northern Area 8 a.m. - 2 p.m. Brigade Aquatic Sports at 4 p.m. in the river at HOULLE.	

WAR DIARY
or
INTELLIGENCE SUMMARY.
(Erase heading not required.)

Army Form C. 2118.

Instructions regarding War Diaries and Intelligence Summaries are contained in F.S. Regs., Part II. and the Staff Manual respectively. Title pages will be prepared in manuscript.

Place	Date	Hour	Summary of Events and Information	Remarks and references to Appendices
	22nd.		A & B Coys. fired on "B" Range from 6 – 8 a.m. During the morning Coys. paraded under Coy. arrangements near billets. 100 men per Coy. bathed at HOULLE during the afternoon.	
	23rd.		C & D Coys. fired on "B" Range from 6 – 8 a.m. Coys. paraded under Coy. arrangements during the morning. A warning order was received that the Battalion would move to the WIPPENHOEK area near ABEELE. The Regtl. Transport started today and halted at NOORDPEENE for the night, continuing the march next day. Weather fair.	
	24th.		The Battalion marched out from HOULLE at 9.20 a.m. entrained at WATTEN 1 p.m., detrained from at ABEELE at 4 p.m. and arrived in billets (K.30. & L.25) at about 6.30 p.m. Very crowded and scattered billets. The Division later transferred to II Corps of Second (?)	
	25th.		The Battalion rested during the morning, and cleaned up etc. At 6 p.m. the Battalion was conveyed in 36 motor lorries to DICKEBUSCH HUTS, arriving there about 8 p.m. Transport proceeded by road.	
	26th.		A & B Coys. visited the II Corps model of Corps Front. Parades under Coy. arrangements.	
	27th.		Lieut. Colonel B.C.M. WESTERN, D.S.O., while reconnoitring the trenches the Battalion was to take over was severely wounded by a shell. Major R.C. Grellet assumed command of the Battalion. C & D Coys. visited the II Corps Model. Other parades under Coy. arrangements - arms drill, gas drill, ceremonial etc. At 5 p.m. orders were received to vacate the camp by 8.30 p.m. and take over an area near CHATEAU SEGARD. During the move it rained very heavily and bivouacs were erected with great difficulty. 1½ Coys. were accommodated in trenches. Others in bivouacs. 2/Lt. J.H. McNicholas and 50 O.Rs. were employed as Yukon Pack Carriers. They lived at the ECOLE YPRES and carried S.A.A., fireworks etc. to the forward dump.	
	28th.		Officers reconnoitred the forward areas. Weather - Rain and high winds.	
	29th.		Reconnoitring parties to the forward areas. 3 casualties to Yukon Pack party. Parades - Arms drill, gas drill, inspections. Weather showery.	
	30th.		As for yesterday. The enemy shelled the camp slightly about midnight. No casualties.	

Army Form C. 2118.

WAR DIARY
or
INTELLIGENCE SUMMARY.
(Erase heading not required.)

Instructions regarding War Diaries and Intelligence Summaries are contained in F. S. Regs., Part II. and the Staff Manual respectively. Title pages will be prepared in manuscript.

Place	Date	Hour	Summary of Events and Information	Remarks and references to Appendices
	31st.		Usual parades. N.C.Os. and Battn. runners reconnoitred the forward areas. Weather fair. No rain.	

A. Green Major,
Commanding 8th. Yorkshire Regiment.

8th. Yorkshire Regiment.

War Diary for September 1917.

Army Form C. 2118.

WAR DIARY
or
INTELLIGENCE SUMMARY.
(Erase heading not required.)

Instructions regarding War Diaries and Intelligence Summaries are contained in F.S. Regs., Part II. and the Staff Manual respectively. Title pages will be prepared in manuscript.

Place	Date	Hour	Summary of Events and Information	Remarks and references to Appendices
FIELD.	September 1917.			
	1st.		Parades in camp. Drill etc. Weather - heavy rain.	
	2nd.		Marched from bivouacs at DICKEBUSCH at 7 am. to billets at STEENVOORDE arriving 1 pm. Weather fine.	
	3rd.		Marched from STEENVOORDE Area to WULVERDINGHE. Started 7 am. - halted at ZUYTPEENE for 2 hours. Arrived in billets 7 pm. Very trying march. Weather hot.	
	4th.		Ordinary parades - Inspections and cleaning up. Weather fine.	
	5th.		Parades under Coy. arrangements. Weather very fine.	
	6th.		Usual parades. Cricket match Officers v. Sergeants. Officers won by 4 runs. Heavy rain in evening.	
	7th.		Parades under Coy. arrangements. Weather fine.	
	8th.		Parades under Coy. arrangements. Battalion played Brigade team at cricket and won by 40 runs.	
	9th.		The whole of the battalion were on the range including Lewis Guns. 120 men bathed at ST.MOMELIN. Weather fine.	
	10th.		Battalion marched to X Corps Training Ground. Officers, N.C.Os and specialists looked over an area which had been marked out to simulate the actual ground over which the Battalion will attack. Intensive digging was practised.	
	11th.		Usual parades in billets. Football match Officers v. Sergeants - Offs. 1. Sgts. 4. goals.	
	12th.		Practice attack by the Brigade on the Training area. General Sir. Herbert C.O. Plumer G.C.M.G. G.C.V.O. K.C.B. A.D.C. attended. C Company Bathed	
	13th.		Marched to STEENVOORDE - 4 stragglers. The distance was 20 miles. Arrived at 7 pm.	
	14th.		Marched to ALBERTA Camp near REMINGHELST. Arrived at 2 pm.	
	15th.		Parades under Coy. arrangements. Coys. practised forming up on tapes at dawn. Weather fine.	

Army Form C. 2118

WAR DIARY
or
~~INTELLIGENCE~~ SUMMARY

(Erase heading not required.)

Instructions regarding War Diaries and Intelligence Summaries are contained in F.S. Regs., Part II. and the Staff Manual respectively. Title Pages will be prepared in manuscript.

Place	Date	Hour	Summary of Events and Information	Remarks and references to Appendices
	16th.		Battalion moved to MICMAC CAMP. Hostile planes over the camp. Weather good.	
	17th.		300 men bathed at Dickebusch. Parades at dawn to practise forming up on tapes. The usual reconnoitring parties went up the line. Battle stores were issued.	
	18th.		Remainder of battle stores issued. G.O.C. Brigade addressed the battalion on the forthcoming operations. Parades as usual.	
	19th.		A & D Coys. left MICMAC CAMP at 1 p.m. for the line. B & C Coys. and H.Q. left MICMAC CAMP at 7.30 p.m. for the line. Weather - rained from 8.30 p.m. - 12 midnight.	
	20th. to 24th.		69th. Brigade attacked INVERNESS COPSE at 5.45 a.m. A Coy. moved into NEW CUT at zero plus 15 minutes. At 2.30 p.m. ordered to report to O.C. 10th. Duke of Wellington's Regt. and were ordered by him to proceed to S.P. "N" and support right of GREEN LINE. Two platoons dug in in front of S.P. "N" and at dusk 2/Lieut. Summerville with 2 Lewis Gun Sections were attached to O.C. A Coy, 10th. Duke of Wellington's Regt. These dispositions remained unchanged until Coy. was relieved. On night of 21st. C Coy. relieved the front line Coy. of the Dukes. D. of W's. for attack on final objective just referred to. D Coy. Was attached to 10th. D. of W's. for attack on final objective. Moved to Clapham Junction - Stirling Castle area on night of 19/20th. where Coy. lay out in the open behind ridge until zero on the 20th. when they moved into E JASPER LANE, where they remained till zero plus 3 hrs. They then advanced with the Australian Division on their left and the Duke of Wellington's on their right, and took the final objective at about 11 a.m. where the Coy. consolidated. Enemy attempted no counter attack and the Coy. was finally relieved by D Coy, 9th. Yorks. on night 23/24th. C Coy. At 11.30 a.m. the Company moved up to the BLUE LINE to act as reserve to GREEN LINE. At 6.30 a.m. on the 21st. the Coy. relieved B & C Coys. of the 10th. Duke of Wellington's Regt. in the front line. On the 22nd. the Coy. was relieved by the Sherwood Foresters at 9.30 p.m. and moved to SANCTUARY WOOD. The Coy. was relieved by the 4th. Suffolk Regt. on the morning of the 24th. inst. B Coy. The night before the offensive B Company rested at WELLINGTON CRESCENT trench on YEOMANRY RIDGE arriving there at about 11 p.m. The following morning (Sept.20) the Coy. was ordered to move to the assembly positions in NEW CUT at Zero plus 15 minutes, carrying with them the consolidation stores. On arrival at assembly positions more stores were drawn. At zero plus 3 hours, B Company followed the West Riding Regt. over the top, moving in half	

1875. Wt. W593/826 1,000,000 4/15 J.B.C. & A. A.D.S.S./Forms/C. 2118.

Army Form C. 2118.

WAR DIARY
or
INTELLIGENCE SUMMARY.
(Erase heading not required.)

Instructions regarding War Diaries and Intelligence Summaries are contained in F.S. Regs., Part II. and the Staff Manual respectively. Title pages will be prepared in manuscript.

Place	Date	Hour	Summary of Events and Information	Remarks and references to Appendices
			platoons in artillery formation. The barrage laid down by the enemy on INVERNESS COPSE was passed through with some casualties and the company reached its objective at the four dugouts near the TOWER (S.P. "U"). These dugouts were found to be destroyed, and the Coy. dug in round them, forming a strong point. Reconnoitring parties proceeded to the GREEN LINE at NORTHAMPTON FARM, and strong point "O" to find out the situation and the positions of the Coys. capturing the GREEN LINE. An hour after arrival at the objective, two platoons were ordered by the C.O. 10th. Duke of Wellingtons Regt to reinforce the GREEN LINE. Nos. 5 & 6 platoons proceeded there and dug in. The remaining two platoons were ordered to proceed to dugouts to form STRONG POINT "U" and act as supports to the GREEN LINE. These two platoons also brought forward the consolidation stores brought over by the Company. During the night of the 20/21st. the platoons in the front line carried on consolidation, and by morning a continuous line had been dug. At 7 p.m. on the 21st. the enemy opened a heavy barrage on the forward area and large numbers of them were seen massing for a counter attack. They were dispersed by artillery and our Lewis Gun fire. More work was carried on during the night of the 21/22nd. on the night of the 22/23rd. the Company was relieved and proceeded to SANCTUARY WOOD CRATERS.) The following day (Sept. 22nd.) the Company was employed as carrying parties and in salvage work on the area behind CLAPHAM JUNCTION - STIRLING CASTLE. The following morning (24th. Sept) the company was relieved and came back to ALBERTA CAMP (near RENINGHELST).	
	25th.		Major R.C.Grellet (actg. C.O.) and Lieut. W.B.Bush, (Adjutant) were wounded on the 22nd. Capt. E.Boys. took over command of the battalio n at 5 a.m. on the 22nd.	
	26th.		The battalion was inspected at ALBERTA CAMP by Major General Sir J.M.Bebington, K.C.M.G., C.B at 3.30 p.m. The remainder of the day was spent in cleaning up.	
			N.C.Os. and men who took part in the operation of the 20th. bathed at WESTOUTRE.	
	27th.		Major A.O.Barnes, D.S.O. took over temporary command of the Battalion. The battalion left ALBERTA CAMP at 9 a.m. and proceeded to SCOTTISH WOOD by bus. Left SCOTTISH WOOD at 2.30 p.m. and marched to SANCTUARY WOOD. Took over line at midnight from about J.16.a.6.7. to J.15.d.5.5. A, B.& D Coys. in the front line; C Coy. in support in a trench in front of and South of BLACK WATCH CORNER, J.15.a.9.9.	
	28th.		Support Coy. were very heavily shelled and suffered casualties. Weather good.	

Army Form C. 2118.

WAR DIARY
or
INTELLIGENCE SUMMARY.
(Erase heading not required.)

Instructions regarding War Diaries and Intelligence Summaries are contained in F. S. Regs., Part II. and the Staff Manual respectively. Title pages will be prepared in manuscript.

Place	Date	Hour	Summary of Events and Information	Remarks and references to Appendices
	29th.		Support Coy. again heavily shelled.	
	30th.		Battalion was relieved by the 9th. Yorkshire Regiment. Relief completed by midnight. Battalion proceeded to the CRATERS near SANCTUARY WOOD. In the early morning there was a very thick mist, but later the weather was magnificent. 30 prisoners and 4 light machine guns were captured during this tour of the trenches.	
			M. Hackhorse	
			Major,	
			Commanding 8th. Yorkshire Regiment.	
	4.10.17.			

8th. Service Battalion A.P.W.O.Yorkshire Regiment.

War Diary.

October 1917.

Army Form C. 2118.

WAR DIARY
or
INTELLIGENCE SUMMARY.
(Erase heading not required.)

Instructions regarding War Diaries and Intelligence Summaries are contained in F. S. Regs., Part II. and the Staff Manual respectively. Title pages will be prepared in manuscript.

Place	Date	Hour	Summary of Events and Information	Remarks and references to Appendices
IN THE FIELD.	OCT. 1917. 1st.		Left the CRATERS, SANCTUARY WOOD, and proceeded to RIDGE WOOD near HALLEBAST CORNER. Major A.C Barnes, D.S.O. relinquished command. Major M.R.C.Backhouse, D.S.O. assumed command of the Battalion.	
	2nd.		Proceeded by bus from RIDGE WOOD to the BRETHEN AREA. R.33.b.5.5. Sheet 28.	
	3rd.		Parades under Coy. arrangements - Kit inspections and general cleaning up. Weather dull but fair.	
	4th.		Parades under Coy arrangements. A & D Coys. proceeded to I.1.b.6.8. north of Ypres to work on construction of a light railway. Weather unsettled.	
	5th.		Parades under Coy. arrangements. Inspections etc. H.Q., B & C Coys. bathed. Draft of 49 O.Rs. arrived from base. Weather wet.	
	6th.		Parades under Coy. arrangements. Weather very wet, interfering with parades.	
	7th.		Brigade Church parade was held in the field behind Battn. Hdqrs. Bishop Gwynne, Bishop of Khartoum took the service. The Commanding Officer and R.S.M. visited A & D Coys North of YPRES. Weather very cold and wet. The billets are very poor and the men are suffering from inclement weather and bad billets.	
	8th.		The Battalion practised a route march for about nine miles in full marching order. One man fell out. Weather magnificent. At night the weather turned very stormy. The Orderly Room tent was blown away.	
	9th.		Received orders to stand by for a move. Parades under Coy. arrangements near billets. The Transport was inspected by the Commanding Officer. A bombing pit was dug near Battn. H.Q. and practice with live bombs was carried out. Received a draft of 5 O.R.	
	10th.		Still standing by for a move. Notification received that Major R.C.Grellet had been awarded the Distinguished Service Order. Received a draft of 23 O.Rs. The Battalion marched from billets at R.33.b.central at 3.5 p.m. and proceeded to ONTARIO CAMP, RENINGHELST.	

Army Form C. 2118.

WAR DIARY
or
INTELLIGENCE SUMMARY.
(Erase heading not required.)

Instructions regarding War Diaries and Intelligence Summaries are contained in F. S. Regs., Part II. and the Staff Manual respectively. Title pages will be prepared in manuscript.

Place	Date	Hour	Summary of Events and Information	Remarks and references to Appendices
	11th.		Parades under Coy. arrangements. Standing by for a move.	
	12th.		The Battalion marched from Ontario Camp at 9.25a.m. and proceeded to a camp near HALLEBAST CORNER, N.2.b.8.7. Sheet28 S.W. A & D Coys. rejoined the Battalion. Weather very stormy and wet.	
	13th.		A & D Coys. bathed at Dickebusch and received a clean change. Inspections by Coy. Commanders - all necessaries for the trenches made up. Weather very wet and stormy. 2/Lieut. C.J. Roddam and 13 O.Rs. reported for duty. Battn. moved to the Bund at noon.	
	14th.		Following wire received from Brigade:- "The Army Commander has desired that his appreciation of the conduct of all ranks of the 23rd. Division during the operations from 27.9.17. to 2.10.17 should be conveyed to all Units concerned. The manner in which the several line was held and the several counter attacks replused reflects great credit on all the troops engaged." Battalion went into support. H.Q. C & D Coys. at the Bund, A & B Coys at Railway Dugouts, under orders of the 68th. Brigade. Trench Strength - 17 Off. and 521 O.R. Details - 6 Off. and 161 O.Rs. proceeded to MICMAC CAMP at H.31.b.4.0. Draft of 9 O.Rs. reported. Weather fine.	
	15th.		Transport transferred from camp at N.2.b.6.7. to I.25.a. Parades for details 9 a.m. - 12 noon. Classes under R.S.M. Lieut. Millhouse and 2/Lt. Dudley. General Training. Lieut. H.L.Oakley and 2/Lieut. D.Fullerton reported for duty. The Battalion relieved the 10th. Northumberland Fusiliers in the front line on the night of 15/16th. The relief was very well carried out, and there were only two casualties. Two companies 10th. Northumberland Fusiliers remained in support at about J.10.c.70.75, and J.10.c.80.15. Sheet 28 N.E.3.	
	16th.		The dispositions of the companies were as follows:- (Sheet 28 N.E.3.) Front Line:- B Coy on the left flank at J.11.c.9.3.; C Coy. in the centre at about J.11.c.40.50.; A Coy. on the right flank at about J.10.d.90.30.; D Coy. in immediate support at J.11.c.central. During the day there was a great deal of movement noticed in the enemy's lines, particularly about the railway line running over the far crest on a bearing from J.11.c.9.3. of 145 Mag. A large stretch of the line, was visible from the front trenches and trams were seen moving on it.	

Army Form C. 2118.

WAR DIARY
or
INTELLIGENCE SUMMARY.
(Erase heading not required.)

Instructions regarding War Diaries and Intelligence Summaries are contained in F. S. Regs., Part II. and the Staff Manual respectively. Title pages will be prepared in manuscript.

Place	Date	Hour	Summary of Events and Information	Remarks and references to Appendices
	16th.		This information was notified to Brigade by Pigeon post, but so far as we could ascertain, no action was taken by the Artillery. Hostile aircraft were very active all day and at intervals came down very low and fired at various parties of our men. Very few of our aeroplanes were seen The enemy's artillery were active all day. Details - Training - General and special under O.C.Details (69th.Bde) 9 a.m. - 12.30 p.m. A draft of four other ranks reported for duty. Weather cold and showery.	
	17th.		Hostile artillery barrage very heavy through the night especially on our immediate support about J.11.c.central. During the night owing to the enemy shelling very little work could be done. Enemy aircraft was very active, especially during the early morning. "A" Coy. sent out a daylight patrol which reconnoitred the road running south from J.17.a.20.75. without encountering any of the enemy. Hostile artillery activity continued throughout the day. Patrols were sent out to get in touch with the unit on our left, but were not successful. Touch was obtained with the 10th. Durham Light Infantry, XIV Division on our right. Details - General and special training under O.C.Details, 69th.Bde. 9a.m.- 12.30p.m. 2/Lieut. N.Miller arrived from England.	
	18th.		Bosche aeroplanes were active during the morning, flying at a low altitude over our front trenches. There was very little hostile shelling on this front during the day, but at night the enemy shelled continuously from 6 p.m. - 6 a.m. 19th.inst. On the night of the 18/19th.inst, we were relieved by the 13th. Durham Light Infantry, but owing to the severe shelling the relief was very difficult to carry out. The relief was completed by about 7 a.m. on the 19th. B & C Coys. relieved the two Coys. of the 10th. Northumberland Fusiliers in support. During the relief there was very heavy shelling, but fortunately C Coy. got through with only three casualties (slight), B Coy. did not finish relief until dawn, and had one man killed and several wounded. Their positions at J.10.c.80.15 was a bad one, and was shelled very heavily the whole time our Coy. was there. C Coy. was in good dugouts at J.10.c.70.75. 69th. Brigade details Camp removed from MICMAC CAMP to BURGOMASTER FARM close to DICKEBUSCH LAKE (Sheet 28 N.W.) H.34.a.5.2. Weather fine. 2/Lieut. E.Clegg struck off the strength having been transferred to the Royal Engineers.	
	19th.		H.Q., A & D Coys. marched to N.2.b.6.7. near HALLEBAST CORNER, and went into camp there under orders of the G.O.C. 70th. Brigade. A draft of four other ranks reported for duty.	

Army Form C. 2118.

WAR DIARY
or
INTELLIGENCE SUMMARY.
(Erase heading not required.)

Instructions regarding War Diaries and Intelligence Summaries are contained in F. S. Regs., Part II. and the Staff Manual respectively. Title pages will be prepared in manuscript.

Place	Date	Hour	Summary of Events and Information	Remarks and references to Appendices
	20th.		H.Q., A & D Coys. and details who were left out of the line entrained at WIZERNES and marched to ACQUIN arriving about 8 p.m. B & C Coys. were relieved in the support line by 2 Coys. by 2 Coys. of the 1st. Bn. East Yorkshire Regiment, and proceeded to a camp at I.20.b.	
	21st.		B & C Coys. embussed at 10 a.m. and proceeded to ACQUIN under orders of G.O.C. 68th. Bde. and rejoined the Battalion. The casualties in the line were as follows:- Lieut. C.H.Sparshott wounded (at duty); 2/Lieut. T.E.Hardcastle wounded (accidentally); other ranks - 32 killed, 1 missing, 45 wounded. Church parade was held in the Transport Field at 11.30 a.m. Battalion came under orders of the 69th. Brigade.	
	22nd.		Parades under Coy. arrangements. Kit inspections, cleaning up etc. Weather wet. Notification was received that the following had been awarded decorations for gallantry in the field. Bar to Military Medal - 7650 Cpl. E.Fellows, A Coy.; 11289 Pte. W.Thompson, D Coy; 13607 Pte. J.Rudd, B Coy; 18630 Pte. F.McLean, A Coy; Military Medal - 201485 Pte. S.Dickinson, C Coy; 42867 Pte. H.Middleton, C Coy; 42628 Pte. T. Bel Blackburn, D Coy; 16101 Pte. H.Dobson, D Coy; 13652 Cpl. S.Burdon, D Coy; 14771 Cpl. G.R.H. Laing, B Coy; 14865 Pte. J.McNay, B Boy; 38578 Pte. A.Walker, D Coy; 13377 Pte. J.P.Hughes, D Coy; 53310 L/C. R.Ager, A Coy; 14876 Pte. S.Buckton, C Coy; 25951 Cpl. J.Gamble, B Coy. 10872 L/C J. Hill, B Coy; 30474 Pte. J.W.Drury, D Coy; 16299 Pte. R.Dowie, C Coy; 16739 Cpl. T.Young, D Coy; 27279 Pte. E.L.Curry, C Coy; 49464 Pte. W.Smith, B Coy; 241623 Pte. J.M.Dowey, D Coy; 13883 L/C W.Crake, A Coy;11551 Cpl. A.Turner, C Coy; 12361 Sgt. J.P.Appleton, A Coy; 13986 Pte. J.Orton, A Coy; 13874 Pte. H.Sewell, A Coy;	
	23rd.		Parades under Coy. arrangements. The following officers joined the Battalion - 2/Lieut. L.Hart posted to A Coy; 2/Lieut. K.C.Bruce, posted to B Coy; 2/Lieut. H.Oldfield and 2/Lieut. F. Summerscale posted to D Coy. Draft of 5 O.R. arrived.	
	24th.		Parades under Coy. arrangements. Notification received that the following had been awarded decorations for gallantry in the Field. Military Cross - Capt. E.Boys, Capt. J.Tilly, Capt. F.G.Miller, 2/Lieut. C.T.Hepworth. Distinguished Conduct Medal - 15201 Cpl. A.Danby, C Coy. Military Medal.- 42367 Pte. J.C.Downie, C Coy; 17804 Pte. W.Hendry, C Coy.	
	25th.		The G.O.C. 23rd. Division presented Medal Ribbons awarded to Officers and men of the Battalion.	

Army Form C. 2118.

WAR DIARY
or
INTELLIGENCE SUMMARY.
(Erase heading not required.)

Instructions regarding War Diaries and Intelligence Summaries are contained in F. S. Regs., Part II. and the Staff Manual respectively. Title pages will be prepared in manuscript.

Place	Date	Hour	Summary of Events and Information	Remarks and references to Appendices
	25th.		The undermentioned officers and men ewere decorated:-	
			Capt. E.Boys. Capt. J.Tilly. 2/Lieut. C.T.Hepworth.	
			7650 Cpl. E.Fellowes, A Coy. 11289 Pte. W.Thomson, D Coy. 13607 Pte. J.Rudd. B Coy.	
			18630 Pte. F.McLean, A Coy. 201485 Pte.S.Dickinson, C Coy. 30474 Pte. J.W.Drury. D Coy.	
			42367 Pte. J.C.Downie. C Coy. 17804 Pte. W.Hendry, C Coy. 42867 Pte. H.Middleton. C Coy.	
			42628 Pte.T.Blackburn. D Coy. 16739 Cpl. T.Young, D Coy. 16101 Pte. H.Dobson. D Coy.	
			27279 Pte. E.L.Curry. C Coy. 14771 Cpl. G.R.H.Laing. B Coy. 29464 Pte. W.Smith. B Coy.	
			14865 Pte. J.McNay, B Coy. 241623 Pte. J.M.Dowey, D Coy. 28578 Pte. A.Walker. D Coy.	
			13885 L/C.W.Crake, A Coy. 13377 Pte. J.P.Hughes, D Coy. 11551 Cpl. A.Turner, C Coy.	
			12361 Sgt. J.P.Appleton. A Coy. 29591 Cpl. J.Gamble, B Coy. 13874 Pte. H.Sewell, A Coy.	
			C Coy played B Coy in the inter-Coy. football competition. Result - C Coy 8 goals. B Coy NIL.	
	26th.		Parades under Coy. arrangements. In the afternoon H.Q.Staff played D Coy. Result - D Coy 1, H.Q. 4 goals.	
	27th.		The whole battalion bathed at the baths at ACQUIN. Every man received a clean change. In the afternoon A Coy fired on the range.	
	28th.		A special service in memory of the following members of the Battalion who were killed in recent actions was held in the Transport Field at 9.30 a.m.	
			2/Lieut. H.Bell.	
			20663 Pte. J.Welsh. 49435 Pte. B.Collinge. 33589 Pte. W.Lowerson. 28113 Sgt. A Collins	
			241786 Pte. J.Rodgers. 202034 Pte. W.Smailes. 42883 Pte. A.Reed. 20459 Pte. T.Scott.	
			15212 Pte. W.White. 200179 Pte. E.W.Brand. 45733 Pte. A.Harrison. 13786 Sgt.G.Fearnley.	
			42646 Pte. G.H.Hall. 11494 Pte. G.W.Smith. 19393 L/Sgt.R.Jackson. 12495 Pte. L.Potts.	
			41467 Pte. S.Sobrell. 11423 Pte. R.Dodds. 25648 Pte. R.Smith. 12836 Pte.R.Finlay.	
			45804 Pte. R.Graham. 11848 Pte. R.Butson. 23599 L/C. G.Milner. 17493 Pte.H.McKeown.	
			33640 Pte. B.C.Pierson. 241476 Pte. R.Pearson. 12110 Sgt. T.Williams. 42814 Pte. R.Betts.	
			200518 Pte. A.Bruce. 26237 Pte. F.T.Shields. 201825 Pte. F.Sturdy. 240849 Pte.W.Best.	
			203184 Pte. G.Alliss. 15752 Pte. J.Kelly. 19394 Pte. E.Brown. 45814 Pte. W.Tate.	
			53614 Pte. S.A.Collins. 18620 Pte. R.Morris. 29171 Pte. W.Morton. 49454 Pte.G.Crowe.	
			29295 Pte. M.Whitehead. 42591 Pte. J.Waddington. 39262 Pte. J.McCarthy. 18062 Cpl.H.Greener.	
			23415 Pte. N.Gilbert. 38835 Pte. H.Ashton. 41995 Pte. H.Hardy. 11460 Pte.R.Ramsay.	

Army Form C. 2118.

WAR DIARY
or
INTELLIGENCE SUMMARY.
(Erase heading not required.)

Instructions regarding War Diaries and Intelligence Summaries are contained in F.S. Regs., Part II. and the Staff Manual respectively. Title pages will be prepared in manuscript.

Place	Date	Hour	Summary of Events and Information	Remarks and references to Appendices
	28th.		20322 Pte. C.Patterson. 242552 Pte. J.Wright. 34159 Pte. T.Brennan. 242736 Pte. J.Noble.	
			19118 Pte. F.Wilcocks. 14610 Sgt. Hampshire H. 42871 Pte. W.Neil. 42643 Pte. H.Dyson.	
			45789 Pte. R.Weatherill. 15545 Pte. J.Kelly. 22823 Pte. J.Lofthouse. 42001 Pte. T.Parker.	
			241134 Pte. T.E.Richardson. 38230 Pte. J.Chorlton. 200490 Pte. G.Akers. 28210 Pte. R.Speight.	
			41306 Pte. H.Whitehouse. 33604 Pte. F.W.Boden. 41619 Pte. E.Fletcher. 28202 Pte. J.Place.	
			27241 Pte. G.Easton. 14933 Pte. E.O'Brien. 235400 Pte. J.W.Brown. 15036 Pte. J.Mather.	
			42816 Pte. A.Brown. 235410 Pte. T.M.Douglas. 49429 Pte. F.Beard. 34148 Pte. G.Milling.	
			34140 Pte. L.Swindles. 10872 Cpl. J.Hill. 34160 Pte. J.Clark. 24177 Pte. W.Bishop.	
			13986 Pte. J.Orton. 202942 Pte. J.Hardy. 16735 L/Sgt. J.McManus. 10757 Pte. J.Sharp.	
			13769 Pte. M.Smith. 19792 Pte. T.Parker. 18648 Pte. M.Raw. 42645 Pte. H.Holdsworth.	
			29196 Pte. W.Farrar. 29166 Pte. W.Clayton. 42896 Pte. E.Williams. 36282 Pte. W.Berry.	
			13867 Pte. M.Gibbons. 10538 Pte. S.Smith. 29741 Pte. T.Langley. 33053 Pte. J.Dinsdale.	
			33411 Pte. W.Etherington. 42618 Pte. T.Beevers. 19796 Cpl. J.W.Priestley. 42002 Pte. J.Roberts.	
			The Commanding Officer inspected billets, cookers, etc. 2/Lieut. L.Hart and 4 N.C.Os. left	
			to undergo a course of P. & B.T. Received warning orders to be ready to move by rail at once.	
			Destination unknown.	
			Capt. R.G.Atkinson and 2Lieut. A.T.Dudley reported from course.	
	29th.		Inspection of the Battalion By Major General Sir J.M.Babington, K.C.M.G., C.B. at BOISDINGHEM.	
			Battalion gave General Salute and were then inspected by Major General Sir J.M.Babington,	
			K.C.M.G., C.B. after which the Battalion marched past in column of route.	
			Weather fine.	
	30th.		Inspection by the Commanding Officer. Otherwise parades under Coy. arrangements. Weather	
			cold and wet. 2/Lieut. F.G.Parker and three other ranks reported for duty.	
	31st.		The Battalion paraded at 9.30 a.m. in drill order and marched to LEULINGHEM where the Brigade	
			was formed up for inspection by Field Marshal Sir Douglas Haig, K.T., G.C.B., G.C.V.O., G.C.I.E.	
			Commander-in-Chief, British Armies in France. Strength for parade 26 Off. 540 Other ranks.	
			Brigade gave the General Salute, after which the Brigade marched past in Column of companies.	
			The Commander-in-Chief expressed his great appreciation to the Commanding Officer on the	
			turn out, arms movements, and the way in which the Battalion marched past.	

Army Form C. 2118.

WAR DIARY
or
INTELLIGENCE SUMMARY.
(Erase heading not required.)

Place	Date	Hour	Summary of Events and Information	Remarks and references to Appendices
	31st.		Total reinforcements received during the month - 9 Officers and 107 other ranks. Total admissions to Hospital sick during the month - 4 Officers and 49 Other ranks. Strength of the Battalion on this date - 43 Officers and 803 other ranks. Wanting to complete on this date - 168 other ranks.	

J. Backhouse
Lieut.Colonel,
Commanding 8th. Yorkshire Regiment.

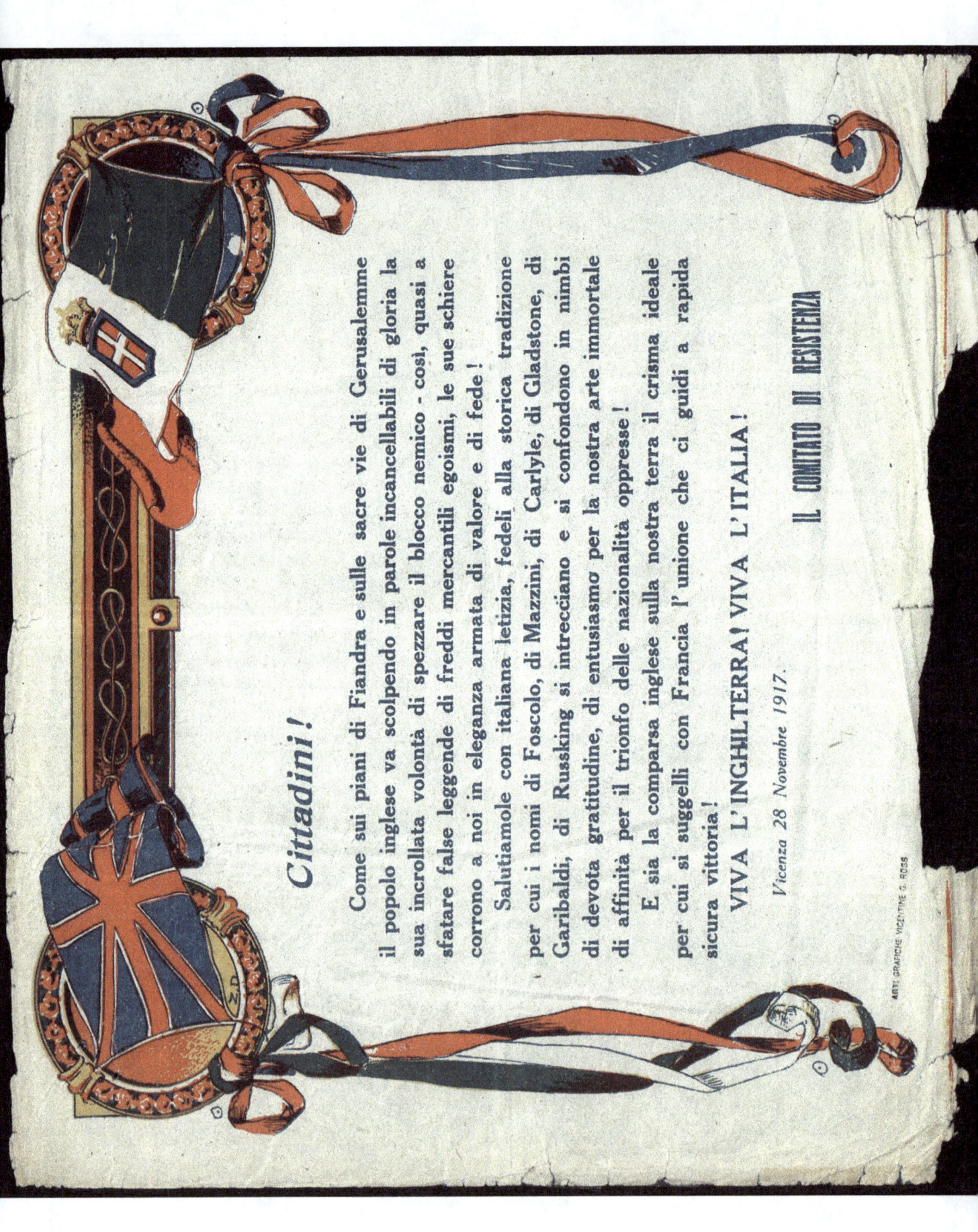

Cittadini!

Come sui piani di Fiandra e sulle sacre vie di Gerusalemme il popolo inglese va scolpendo in parole incancellabili di gloria la sua incrollata volontà di spezzare il blocco nemico – così, quasi a sfatare false leggende di freddi mercantili egoismi, le sue schiere corrono a noi in eleganza armata di valore e di fede!

Salutiamole con italiana letizia, fedeli alla storica tradizione per cui i nomi di Foscolo, di Mazzini, di Carlyle, di Gladstone, di Garibaldi, di Russking si intrecciano e si confondono in nimbi di devota gratitudine, di entusiasmo per la nostra arte immortale di affinità per il trionfo delle nazionalità oppresse!

E sia la comparsa inglese sulla nostra terra il crisma ideale per cui si suggelli con Francia l'unione che ci guidi a rapida sicura vittoria!

VIVA L'INGHILTERRA! VIVA L'ITALIA!

Vicenza 28 Novembre 1917.

IL COMITATO DI RESISTENZA

TO MY BRITISH AND FRENCH COMRADES

Allow one of your Italian companions, one who has lived in your countries for many years and has learnt to appreciate you, to express in the name of his Italian brothers and for himself their friendship to you and make you feel that, in this season of good-will towards mankind, you find yourselves among sincere friends. We are bound together by a sacred tie fighting as we are for the good of humanity. We intend securing a lasting peace in the world, a peace that will allow our children's children to enjoy unmolested, in the midst of fruitful industry, their patch of sunshine. There's no doubt we'll get what we are striving for.

I am glad you have come over to my country because you will now have the opportunity of knowing it better than you did. I want you to learn to care for us as I learnt to care for you while I lived in France and England. Our three countries and the other generous nations which are siding with us must be welded together for ever in a lasting bond which will represent in the world liberty-loving humanity and be a guarentee that those weaker than ourselves will always have their rights respected and be treated with justice. Live and let live.

But, friends, we three were bound together even before now. A war was not required to unite us in spirit. In the past we have aided one another spontaneously. For ages at a time we have been connected intellectually and the remarkable fact is that only we three met in the region of thought and that the rest of the world afterwards learnt from us the meaning of the word liberty. The German people are our pupils but their leaders have not understood the love for humanity which Shakespeare symbolizes. It was in Italy, in the Dark Ages, about 650 years ago, that a great movement, called the humanistic movement, was started. It was the voice of Dante that first pleaded for mankind. Other Italian writers following Dante spread in the world this spirit which revived human thought, began a new worship of beauty, a new worship of knowledge and a new statesmanship. It is on this movement that modern civilization is founded. From Italy it passed to France and England. Chaucer and Shakespeare, Montaigne and Rabelais absorbed this spirit and made it English and French. This spirit, reawakened by the great French Revolution, was diffused in the world in new forms. And it is this spirit, the expression of ever-lasting civilization, as unextinguishable as are beauty and justice, which now arises again, the source of the new happy age which we look towards with confidence though it appear on the most blood-red horizon in history. This is but one instance, comrades, in which we were united in the past. Since then there has been a continual exchange of thought between France, England and Italy.

Your countries have become powerful and have attracted the admiration of the world because they have existed as States for over a thousand years. It was only less than sixty years ago that the Italians became a united and free Nation. Before Italy was considerd a « geographical expression » consisting, as it did, of a series of small states and petty kingdoms. We were dominated in the north by the Austrians, our natural enemy. But Mazzini, Garibaldi and Cavour dreamed of a united Peninsula. Their dream, aided by France and encouraged by England, and notwithstanding almost unsurmountable obstacles, was in time realised. In 1848 the hated Austrian rule began to be broken and from then to 1866 insurrections and wars cemented with blood the various states and formed the United Kingdom of Italy under the benign rule of the House of Savoy. We have only had a breathing space of little more than fifty years to attend to the peaceful work of art, industry and commerce. Look around you, my friends, and you will see that we have accomplished much for so short a time.

You see I am proud of Italy, but love for one's country is a natural feeling which does not hinder one appreciating other countries. I have studied and admired England and France and that is what I would like you to do with reference to Italy. Now that you are here, and very welcome you are, try to understand us, become interested in Italy, see what we have done and are doing. Don't take us for a race of romantic people, as some modern novelists have thought best to picture us, but consider us for what we are — a great ancient nation grown young again, full of the modern and positive spirit of progress and ever vital. When we all return to the home fires kept burning for us, we must not forget the old acquaintance made. The ties of the Past and the Present must be binding for the Future. That is what I have tried to tell you.

Though the voices of our beloved ones at home do not sound in our ears now, we know that their loving thoughts are always with us. It is for their ultimate happiness that we are making sacrifices. Let this thought be a joy for us.

In the name of my Italian brothers I send you, friends, the old but ever pleasing wish « A Merry Xmas and a Happy New Year ».

Yours very sincerely
Private **Mario Hazon**

Italy, Xmas, 1917.

11 W York Rgt
Vol 26

WAR DIARY or INTELLIGENCE SUMMARY
Army Form C. 2118

Place	Date	Hour	Summary of Events and Information	Remarks and references to Appendices
EDIFIZIO	Dec 1		Battalion in billets at EDIFIZIO. Company and Battalion training. O.C. companies proceed to line in advance of Battalion taking over sector.	
MONTELLO SECTOR	2nd		Battalion moved into line and relieved the 135th Regiment 70th Italian Division. Two companies between R.PIAVE and IL MONTELLO. Right company without Casualties. Battalion in the line. (Right half batt. of 33rd D. manned front.) Line taken over consisted of a system of well made trenches but very little protection against Heavy shell fire. Work commenced on H.Q. of making dug-outs + improving system. Also Battle H.Q. A.B. & C Coys in front line. D Coy in reserve. H.Q. at house 33 near H7/12.	
	3rd 15		Slight enemy shelling on 3rd + 4th. 1 O.R. wounded on 4th. Frontline shelled on 5th about 10 a.m. 1 O.R. killed + 3 O.R. wounded. Artillery seemed actively increased daily during this period. Battalion was in line. On the 9th our Artillery registered on points for S.O.S. Barrage. Results good. On 8 + 9th Patrols were out. On 9th Patrol reconnoitred crossing River ... ... over April days.	

Army Form C. 2118.

WAR DIARY
or
INTELLIGENCE SUMMARY.
(Erase heading not required.)

Instructions regarding War Diaries and Intelligence Summaries are contained in F. S. Regs., Part II. and the Staff Manual respectively. Title pages will be prepared in manuscript.

Place	Date	Hour	Summary of Events and Information	Remarks and references to Appendices
MONTELLO SECTOR	30/6/18		On morning of 9th the XIV Corps commander Rt Honble Earl of Cavan visited M.G. training camp. He was well pleased with the progress made in the out doing and ordinary training + (the bltn received) 14th + 15th had Great + Light howitzer shelling. Battalion relieved by 10th Hampshire holding line left half wing front line + left of Brigade Reserve being billets at VENEGAZZU. Relief completed without casualties. Our casualties during tour in line 14 ORs wounded - 1 OR killed.	
VENEGAZZU	17 16/6/18		Battalion in billets at VENEGAZZU. Reserve bttn moving up. Company training. Bttn HQ & Coys of three battalion in training. Company attended talks on R 79 Many Cen Majors Duff of 110 Otto + three junior Officers on 19 many keen Schemes for approval by Commanding Officers. 20 Lectures on Tactics. the defence of front occupied by 69 Brigade. 3rd Lectures on lecture on 30 38 Lectures by L.O. on tactics employed formerly by action. Lecture by 20 commander of 36 Rapid movement by companies to positions or to 15-16.	

(A800a) D. D. & L., London, E.C.
Wt W.1771/M2031 750,000 5/17 Sch. 92 Forms/C2118/14

Army Form C. 2118.

WAR DIARY
or
INTELLIGENCE SUMMARY.

(Erase heading not required.)

Instructions regarding War Diaries and Intelligence Summaries are contained in F. S. Regs., Part II. and the Staff Manual respectively. Title pages will be prepared in manuscript.

Place	Date	Hour	Summary of Events and Information	Remarks and references to Appendices
VENEGIEZU	26		Ordinary day. Church parade afternoon.	
	26		Company training. D. Coy on Range, Foulkhill Road. Range 27° & 38°.	
	27th		Company training. Bute on 27° & 38° School parade 29°.	
	3P		Battalion Strength. 40 Officers. 1107 O.R.s	

W. Sainsbury
Captain
for Lt Col. Robert of [illegible] Regt.

69th Infantry Brigade.

SPECIAL ORDER OF THE DAY.

After visiting various parts of the Brigade Front today the Commander-in-Chief expressed to the Brigade Commander his high appreciation of all the work done and of the system of defence and desired him to give to all ranks his good wishes for a very happy New Year.

[signature]
Captain.,
Staff Captain.
69th Infantry Brigade.

31/12/17.

XIV Corps G 61/12.
33rd Division G 24/8/4.

7th Division
33rd Division
41st Division

1. The Corps Commander is thoroughly aware of the amount and excellence of the work on defensive lines which has been carried out by all units in the Corps, and has no complaints to make on this head.

2. At the same time, everyone can learn, and he is of opinion that the work done in the Sector held by the 69th Infantry Brigade of the 23rd Division is in advance of anything that is being carried out at the moment, both as regards organisation of labour, and as regards the tactical dispositions.

3. He wishes all units of the Corps to study, and where possible to initiate, the system which is to be seen in this Brigade Sector.
   He wishes therefore, G.S.O.I, and C.R.E of Divisions and all Brigadiers to visit this Sector at as early date as possible, and in any case before January 3rd; the arrangements to be made direct with the G.O.C. 23rd Division.

4. There are many points of interest to be seen. Special attention is called to:-
   (a) The combined action of Machine & Lewis Guns with Trench Mortars in the defence.
   (b) The amount of tunnelling work which is carried out by men who are not trained as tunnellers. Units have complained that they have no tunnellers available, but the G.O.C. 69th Infantry Brigade has clearly proved that tunnellers can be produced from any Unit.
   (c) The excellent interior economy and cleanliness. Every dug out has its rifle rack, in which rifles are standing as clean as if in a barrack room.

5. If it were possible, and can be arranged with the G.O.C. 23rd Division, the Corps Commander would like Battalion Commanders to visit these lines, in addition to the Officers enumerated above.

Signed F. GATHORNE HARDY.
B.G.G.S. XIV Corps

27.12.1917

Certified true copy
31.12.17
Capt/Adjt
11 Bn West Yorkshire Rgt

www.ingramcontent.com/pod-product-compliance
Lightning Source LLC
Chambersburg PA
CBHW081550160426
43191CB00011B/1890